Dancing on the Skillet

Dancing on the Skillet

Ten Truths about Being a School Superintendent

Matthew J. Jennings

ROWMAN & LITTLEFIELD
Lanham • Boulder • New York • London

Published by Rowman & Littlefield
An imprint of The Rowman & Littlefield Publishing Group, Inc.
4501 Forbes Boulevard, Suite 200, Lanham, Maryland 20706
www.rowman.com

6 Tinworth Street, London SE11 5AL, United Kingdom

Copyright © 2021 by Matthew J. Jennings

All rights reserved. No part of this book may be reproduced in any form or by any electronic or mechanical means, including information storage and retrieval systems, without written permission from the publisher, except by a reviewer who may quote passages in a review.

British Library Cataloguing in Publication Information Available

Library of Congress Cataloging-in-Publication Data

Names: Jennings, Matthew, author.
Title: Dancing on the skillet : ten truths about being a school superintendent / Matthew J. Jennings.
Description: Lanham : Rowman & Littlefield, 2021. | Includes bibliographical references. | Summary: "'Ten truths' offers a window into the challenges and possibilities of being a school superintendent. It is a practical account of the realities inherent in the role. Readers will understand the nature of the problems faced as well as practical solutions to obstacles common to the position."—Provided by publisher.
Identifiers: LCCN 2020031784 | ISBN 9781475857849 (cloth) | ISBN 9781475857856 (paperback) | ISBN 9781475857863 (epub)
Subjects: LCSH: School superintendents.
Classification: LCC LB2831.7 .J46 2021 | DDC 371.2/011—dc23
LC record available at https://lccn.loc.gov/2020031784

To Dr. Gerald Woehr and Dr. Karen Harrigan, the two leaders I have known who modeled for me the nature and qualities of true leadership. Thank you.

I also wish to thank Dr. Rick Falkenstein; Nancy Gartenberg; my mother, Jane Jennings; and my wife, MaryAnn Jennings, for the feedback and support they provided me as I have written this book.

Contents

Foreword	ix
Preface	xi
Truth One: The Expectations Others Place upon You Are Unrealistic	1
Truth Two: Change Leadership Is Necessary, but It Is Dangerous Business	9
Truth Three: In General, Teachers Are a Difficult Group to Lead	17
Truth Four: There Is No Such Thing as the "Community"	27
Truth Five: Your "Boss" Is Not Qualified to Do Their Job	35
Truth Six: You Cannot Defeat an Evil, Exploitive Board Majority	43
Truth Seven: There Is a Strong Chance Your Tenure Will Not Last Forever	53
Truth Eight: It Is Lonely at the Top	59
Truth Nine: The Media Do Not Sell the Truth; They Sell Newspapers	65
Truth Ten: You Can Make a Difference	71
Bonus Truths	77
References	79
About the Author	81

Foreword

The role of the superintendent is unique, and everyone's experience is different. Although many articles and books have been written, Dr. Jennings's perspectives are a fresh take valuable to everyone from veteran superintendents to those just entering the field. Despite my twenty years of experience, I am always seeking opportunities to ensure I succeed. Dr. Jennings's candor regarding his current employment is a stark reminder that we are all replaceable, and his "truths" resonate with me and are a reminder of the complexities of the position.

The book's insights regarding communities are certainly true for me. It should serve as another reminder of how quickly we can be replaced and courtesies that we extend can be taken as a right. Navigating the politics of any community is fraught with landmines that may negatively affect the length of one's career.

I too have been in situations when I extend myself and try to do what is right only to have it cause stress and require me to defend my actions. Making assumptions regarding your communities' needs and wants is a dangerous business, as the community is not a single entity and it takes only one person to press their agenda against the community.

The truths that are outlined in the book are intended to help superintendents protect themselves. The field of administration is full of content and ideas to improve your capacity, but this book serves a different purpose. Knowing the truths from Dr. Jennings's perspective can help not only increase the length of your tenure, but it can also protect you from a possible early separation.

Furthermore, he accurately describes the expectations that are placed on school leaders and the need for us to set personal boundaries. The unrealistic expectations placed by the community, board, parents, staff, and politicians leave us with no choice but to set our own limits. Developing a personal sounding board to help set realistic expectations and remember these ten truths are great strategies to improve your professional performance and personal health.

In navigating the role of the superintendent, you quickly realize that there are no right answers. Dr. Jennings has revealed from his personal experience his own truths regarding the position. Although not all these truths may apply to you, the "truth" regarding the position of superintendent can be found only by living the role. However, as you live this role, remember the advice contained in this book, as it will help you navigate the complexities and difficulties we all experience as we try to make education the best it can be for all of our students.

—Dr. Erik Falkenstein

Preface

As I write this, I am on paid administrative leave from my superintendent position. I am not sure how I got here, and I may never know. While I do know that it was not due to illegal or unethical actions on my part, I am not sure what the unresolvable "philosophical differences" were that led to this point.

After sixteen successful years of teaching and administration combined with master's degrees and a doctorate, I assumed the position of superintendent of schools. For eleven years, I worked diligently to improve the quality of education in a school district. In the twelfth year, board elections resulted in a major turnover in the composition of the board. I made efforts to work with the new board members but quickly learned that it was not going to work.

On the one hand, my leave has given me the opportunity to have the time to write this book. On the other, it was a stunning blow to my ego and sense of self. Throughout my time on leave, I have reached out to previous colleagues. Through them and others, I have learned that my negative experience is not uncommon. Perhaps the most unique part of my experience was the actual length of time of my tenure.

In my quest to understand my situation, I read books and articles on the nature of being a superintendent. I discovered many books that articulated the technical aspects for success in the job. However, I did not find much information that shared the real experience of being in the position.

There are so many things I wish I had learned about being a superintendent before I began my tenure. For example, no one ever told me that, by doing the right thing for children, I would develop adversaries. More importantly, no one ever told me how unfair and unethical these adversaries would act to thwart my intentions. Additionally, I did not know how little control I actually had over the things I would be held accountable to achieve.

This book is my attempt to share these "truths" I have learned from both experience and research. It is my hope that it will help current superintendents by validating their experiences. Sometimes, it is valuable to know that you are not alone in what you are experiencing. In addition, hopefully this book will help those considering the superintendent position to make wise and informed choices about pursuing this step in their career. Lastly, I hope that it will help board of education members and members of the public to gain insight into the lives of their superintendents.

The superintendent position is important to the overall quality of a school system. Staff members would have difficulty succeeding without the support of an effective and efficient system. It is also potentially rewarding. There is great satisfaction in knowing that something you did had a major impact on the quality of education provided to children. You can change the future, but it comes at a cost.

The superintendent position is difficult. In addition to all of the technical skills and knowledge required, doing this job well requires strength of character, mental toughness, and a high level of self-awareness. You must know who you are and what you believe in. Not only that; you must also have the fortitude to represent those beliefs in the face of crises and adversity. These are not the things that you learned in graduate school education coursework.

In the chapters that follow, I will articulate ten "truths" about being a superintendent. I will share with you the nature of the problem as well as possible solutions. I do not claim to have identified all of the truths, nor do I believe I can accurately represent the experiences of all superintendents.

Instead, I intend to pass along what I have learned through my research and experience. Additionally, I do not intend to represent my solutions as the only solutions. These are things that have worked for me and others in similar situations. I will share stories, but, to protect anonymity, all of the names and identifying details will be altered.

We begin with the first truth: the expectations for the position are unrealistic, and you will never live up to all of them. While this statement seems bleak, it can actually be liberating. Knowing that the expectations thrust on you as the leader of the school system are unrealistic will help you to resist when others attempt to define you.

Truth One

The Expectations Others Place upon You Are Unrealistic

> The pressures are real, the expectations are high, and the funding is low.
> —Coda and Jetter

HELP WANTED—SUPERINTENDENT OF SCHOOLS

Description

The Anytown USA Board of Education is seeking a miracle worker to lead their school district. This position truly embodies the phrase "do more with less." You will have reduced resources at the same time you will have increased accountability. The community will consist of diverse factions with conflicting expectations, multiple agendas, and changing demographics. You will be expected to compensate for parental apathy, lack of community support, poverty, and dysfunction in homes. You will lead a faculty that is resistant to change, suspicious of authority, and better at working with children than other adults. You will be expected to address the poor performance of those who have greater job security than you, while at the same time keeping morale high. You will report to a group that was elected by a small minority of the total population of the community. These individuals will have no experience doing your job but will evaluate your performance and approve your recommendations. In fact, they will expect you to solve all problems and be responsible for everything from the cleanliness of the bathrooms to increased standardized test scores.

Qualifications

- Advanced degrees, mentoring, and passing standardized exams
- Abundant years of experience in teaching and administration
- Personal qualities, work habits, and leadership skills normally attributed to saints, kings, queens, and presidents
- Willingness to be under the community's magnifying glass for all public behavior
- Teflon skin that allows you to be unfairly criticized on social media, in public meetings, and in newspapers while always maintaining your composure
- Ability to cope with feelings of uncertainty, anxiety, and isolation, especially when facing the inevitable adversity no one has prepared you for

Compensation

You will receive a salary equivalent to that of a midlevel manager in a midsize company. We will provide a multiyear contract. However, if you stir the pot too much, we will either not renew that contract or terminate your employment early. If you are willing to passionately do the hard work required and make difficult decisions that could result in becoming a leper in the educational community, apply today!

CHALLENGES OF UNREALISTIC EXPECTATIONS

Financial and Staff Factors

If we were being honest, this is the classified ad we would use to advertise for most school superintendent positions. A superintendent who approaches the job with passion and courage will face frustration due to problems they have no control over. The public has been led to believe that superintendents have considerable latitude to improve schools.

In fact, most superintendents are surprised by how little real power they have (Ackerman and Maslin-Ostrowski 2002). Traditionally, superintendents are given tremendous responsibility without sufficient authority. This paradox is but one of the problems leading to unrealistic and unattainable expectations for the position.

Another issue is that many states and the federal government are cutting funding to education, while demands for student achievement and staff accountability at all levels are continuing to increase (Evert and Van Deuren 2013). Cuts in funding lead to diminished resources. Perhaps the result is increased class sizes due to staff reductions or elimination of valued but not mandated programs. Maybe the result is elimination of high-quality professional development for staff or elimination of support staff members.

The superintendent does not have the ability to determine the appropriate level of funding a district receives. Instead, the superintendent must work within federal and state regulations, which include multiple unfunded mandates to create a budget that is acceptable to local taxpayers, many of whom express resentment for the tax burden and uninformed opinions of how the money should be spent.

Reductions in funding lead to difficult choices. A superintendent must prioritize the small discretionary portion of the budget on items they believe will lead to the greatest results for children. As with any difficult choice, there will be winners and losers resulting from the outcome. The superintendent will be blamed for the choices that they did not want to have to make in the first place. It is a part of the job, but it is a situation that can only be managed, not won.

In addition, expectations for student achievement continue to increase. With new accountability formulas developed by states, schools are expected to annually demonstrate improvements in standardized test scores. These improvements are measured through assessments whose validity for this purpose is questionable at best. These results are reported and used for comparison and ranking of school districts by a public that does not understand the meaning behind the data.

The actual achievement of annual improvements needs to be accomplished by teachers whose work is largely done in private. Districts do not have the ratio of supervisor to teacher to properly observe most staff. In fact, in most districts less than 1 percent of the time teachers spend doing their work will be observed by a supervisor.

In addition, it is likely that there will be inadequate funding for high-quality professional development for staff. Quality professional development that includes both sufficient time and job-embedded support is costly. Unfortunately, because of its discretionary nature, it is often one of the first cuts to the district budget.

Lastly, the current superintendent probably did not hire most of the current staff members and will not be able to remove those who meet minimum performance standards. Poor performers may be removed, but doing so will come at a great cost in time, effort, legal bills, and negative publicity.

Thus, the superintendent has little control over what occurs in classrooms on a daily basis. They can and must provide a system that supports and enhances the work being done in classrooms and schools. However, most of the outcomes achieved by and attributed to a superintendent are accomplished through the direct efforts of others. If you have a great staff, they will make you look great. Unfortunately, if you have a staff that is mediocre or poor, the opposite will also be true.

Therefore, with limited, highly regulated funding, the superintendent will be held accountable to produce yearly results on questionably valid assessments without having much direct control over the daily work done to achieve those results. Perhaps this would be manageable if communities provided the social capital necessary for schools to succeed.

Community and Parental Factors

Community support plays an important role in the education of children. Yet many communities are characterized by a variety of social ills, such as poverty, abuse, and dysfunctional homes. A superintendent cannot compensate for these factors. A superintendent can do everything within their power to make sure children have the appropriate educational opportunities when they are in the school, but they cannot resolve the larger societal problems and their impact on the schools they lead.

Positive parental involvement has a significant impact on student success (Marzano 2003). Yet what are superintendents expected to do when parents demonstrate apathy for their child's education? They can attempt to enforce policies when students demonstrate significant unexcused absences from school, but usually the damage is already done. They can attempt to hold students accountable for poor behavior choices, but they cannot ensure those messages are appropriately reinforced at home. They can make sure appropriate, meaningful homework assignments are provided, but they cannot supervise completion of that work in the home. Superintendents are implicitly and sometimes explicitly being expected to compensate for larger social problems that they have no control over.

The fact that schools are often the biggest spenders of local taxpayers' dollars and are charged with care and development of the community's children places everything a superintendent does under a microscope. Behaviors that would be normal for others are highly scrutinized.

Everything, including how you dress, how you speak, the car you drive, where you stand or sit at public events, where you eat dinner, and how much you tip the waitress, is being watched carefully. Parents, teachers, and students ascribe meaning to those actions or inactions. For example, a concerned middle school principal shared with me that veteran staff members had been telling people that I walked down only one hallway because that was the hallway containing the "pretty, young" teachers. I guess it never occurred to these veteran teachers that I used this route because it was the only direct one to the main office. This was just one more reminder to me that you are always on stage when you are in the schools or community you serve.

Unfortunately, traditional and public perception of leadership has filtered into the culture of school so much that the community expects and feels entitled to heroic qualities in its administrators (Ackerman and Maslin-Ostrowski 2002). You must appear selfless even when you have unmet personal needs. You must exude confidence and a sense of purpose even when you feel doubt or uncertainty. You must never make mistakes or be inconsistent. You must be unflappable under pressure and in the face of hostility. In short, because you are the big fish in the community's goldfish bowl, you must exhibit superhuman qualities. Unfortunately, while generally hard-working people of good character, superintendents are fallible human beings.

IMPACT ON SUPERINTENDENTS

Several negative things happen to superintendents as a result of these unattainable expectations. First, some superintendents assume the role of the martyr. They will put in seventy-hour work weeks that include weekends. They will sacrifice time with family and friends, including missing their own children's special events to attend school events for other people's children. The belief is that, if they work hard enough and make enough personal sacrifice, they will measure up to the expectations established. Unfortunately, no matter how hard you work or how much you sacrifice, there will be things you cannot fix.

Over time, superintendents who assume the role of the martyr experience adverse effects to their physical and mental health. The stress of trying to meet the expectations of others often leads to poor personal health choices (e.g., weight gain or alcohol consumption) and resentment of others for their lack of appreciation or understanding. As a result of an unsustainable set of work habits, these superintendents eventually lose their effectiveness.

There are two ways to live your life as a superintendent: (1) you can live a balanced life where being a school leader comes after your personal and family priorities, or (2) you can live a life where your career drives everything you do to attempt to prevail. While it is important to put in long hours at times and it is necessary to make some sacrifices to perform your job responsibilities, it is vital to your long-term success that you choose to live a balanced life aligned with your priorities. You will be no good to anyone if you end up sick, constantly angry, or burned out. You must take care of yourself because no one else will.

A second problem resulting from unattainable expectations is self-doubt. When others look to you for solutions to problems you cannot fix, you may come to believe this lack of success is due to some inadequacy on your part. It is you who is to blame and not the situation. In fact, it is usually not you; rather, it is the context of the situation that is the biggest barrier to success. Some problems simply cannot be fixed. No one can solve all of the problems in any school system on their own, especially in a highly political, bureaucratic, and regulated environment.

When experiencing self-doubt, it is common to become overly cautious. Already feeling uncertain, a leader will choose to avoid taking risks. Already feeling unsure, who wants to take actions that may create more potential instability? Yet thoughtful and calculated risk taking as well as what is subsequently learned from those risks is the essence of growth in a school system.

Uncertain leaders will frequently attempt to satisfy others while avoiding conflict. This creates the feeling of stability. However, attempting to satisfy others at the risk of not improving the organization is not leadership. Leaders say and do what they believe must be done while working to manage conflict with others who disagree. These actions require confidence that you can handle the outcomes of this type of situation.

A healthy amount of uncertainty can be important. It can lead to a continuing search for personal and professional growth. Finding a balance between self-doubt and confidence in your knowledge and skills is important. A superintendent must develop the confidence in the belief that they can successfully make substantial changes that will improve the quality of education children receive. This belief must be combined with the humility of knowing you can neither do it alone nor know everything. The greatest gift a superintendent can bestow upon the school district they serve is to ensure that it is substantially better when they leave than when they began their tenure.

Lastly, when we strive to meet others' expectations, we can lose sight of who we are as leaders. Most superintendents would agree that the role requires occasional method acting. Neither do I like wearing a suit, nor do I like being in the spotlight at public events. Yet these are expectations for the role I play, so I fill them. I do not resist these expectations because they do not force me to violate my core values.

Referring back to the previous example of the hallway I used, I refused to change my route because of the false assumptions of others. I value efficiency and logic. Therefore, I would not allow myself to take a circuitous route that would require additional time and not make any sense. Regardless of how this action was being interpreted by others, I was unwilling to change my behavior.

The most important thing a leader needs is a strong sense of self. To navigate difficult circumstances and make tough decisions, a leader needs to know what they believe in and stand for. At the end of the day, you will need to be able to look in the mirror and like what you see. If you think you can fool the reflection looking back at you, then you are a fool.

CONCLUSION

This chapter has established that the expectations for superintendents are unrealistic and therefore are unattainable. Increased accountability combined with reduced resources, community and home factors beyond the school's control, and social expectations for superintendents combine to make the expectations for performance impossible. As a result, some superintendents attempt to adapt by becoming martyrs. Martyrdom does not usually end well for the martyr.

In addition, superintendents can experience self-doubt. This self-doubt can be productive if it spurs motivation for personal and professional growth. It is counterproductive if the superintendent seeks stability by avoiding risks that are necessary for the growth of the school system. The next chapter will expand upon the necessity for leading change while explaining how change leadership will likely damage your career.

KEY POINTS OF THE CHAPTER

- The superintendent will be blamed for the choices that he or she did not want to have to make in the first place. It is a part of the job, but it is a situation they can only manage, not win.
- The superintendent has little control over what occurs in classrooms on a daily basis.
- Superintendents are implicitly and sometimes explicitly being expected to compensate for the larger social problems that they have no control over.
- While generally hard-working people of good character, superintendents are fallible human beings.
- While it is important to put in long hours at times and necessary to make some sacrifices to perform your job responsibilities, it is vital to your long-term success that you choose to live a balanced life aligned with your priorities.
- A superintendent must develop the confidence to believe they can successfully make substantial changes that will improve the quality of education children receive combined with the humility of knowing they can neither do it alone nor know everything.
- At the end of the day, a superintendent will need to be able to look in the mirror and like what they see.

QUESTIONS FOR DISCUSSION OR REFLECTION

1. With the unrealistic and unattainable expectations of the position, you cannot do it all.

a. What do you or will you seek to accomplish as a superintendent?
   b. What is your professional vision for high-quality schools?
   c. What is your mission that will serve to guide your decision-making and the actions you take?

2. What are your core values, and how will you respond to others' expectations if they conflict with those values?

Truth Two

Change Leadership Is Necessary, but It Is Dangerous Business

> Sooner or later a true leader is going to stir the pot.
> —Ackerman and Maslin-Ostrowski

At a public meeting, the board of education expressed concern about district grading practices. They heard multiple complaints from parents about grading inconsistencies between teachers, and some had experienced these discrepancies with their own children. Because the regional high school used these grades as one source of data for high school course placement, it was concluded by board members that our grades needed to be more accurate and consistent. I was tasked with researching and recommending suggestions for changing the district grading policy.

A committee of teachers and administrators was formed to address this task. We read books and articles on this topic. In addition, we reviewed patterns of grade distributions and conducted staff surveys. At the conclusion of our work, the committee recommended seven changes to our policy. These changes were adopted unanimously by the board of education.

Understandably, the teachers on the committee did not want to present these changes to the faculty. They knew the changes would be met with some skepticism. Thus, it was my responsibility to communicate the changes to the staff. I prepared and presented a thorough, detailed presentation that explained the nature and rationale for the changes.

Through examples, I communicated how the changes would lead to a more valid communication of student progress. While I could sense the mood of my audience was not one of enthusiasm, at the conclusion of my presentation I received no comments, questions, or concerns.

Over the course of the next few days, I became aware of rumblings among the faculty about how these changes were causing us to lower our standards. For example, students could no longer receive a zero for an assignment. Instead, the minimum grade to be entered was a 50 out of 100. Despite being shown how skewed grades become by the use of zeros, the accusation was made that, for any number of false reasons, we were lowering our academic standards.

Another example was that, if a retake of a quiz or test were offered, the two grades would no longer be averaged to assign a new score. Instead, the most recent assessment score would be used. The logic was that the more recent score on the assessment of the same content now represented students' knowledge level. After all, the purpose of the grade was to accurately represent what students know and can do.

Staff rumblings made it clear that this was viewed again by some as lowering our standards because it rewarded students for a lack of studying the first time. This was the view, even though it was made clear that retakes were to be provided at the discretion of the teacher. However, if they were to be offered, then they were only to be available to all students who completed some form of remedial work prior to being allowed to complete the retake.

Over a relatively short period of time, social media lit up with complaints about how the district's new grading practices were lowering expectations and standards for our students. These policy changes were blamed for everything from discipline concerns to standardized test score performance and teacher morale issues. Angry letters from concerned parents and community members were sent to the board email account. All types of false accusations were made as reasons for the changes. These accusations consistently included one theme: the superintendent was to blame for these changes.

Thus, an effort to improve the consistency and quality of our communication of student progress had turned into a personal attack on one person. Despite being directed to complete this task by the board and reaching consensus on recommendations with a representative group, the changes were labeled as my idea. This was not the first nor will it be the last time that a superintendent is blamed for a change designed to improve the quality of an aspect of a school system.

CHALLENGES OF CHANGE LEADERSHIP

There are many sound reasons for making changes to how we operate our schools. For example, the rapid pace of change related to the exponential increase in information coupled with the development of new technologies is making it vital for our students to graduate with critical thinking skills and information literacy. Failure to achieve this goal will result in students who are not the effective consumers and producers of this abundance of information.

Globalization and automation are changing the nature of work. Companies are focusing more on providing information than things and are flatter with less hierarchy and less direct supervision. As a result, employees have much more autonomy and responsibility and work in a more collaborative environment. Jobs are less routine, predictable, and stable.

We are currently preparing students for jobs that do not yet exist, using technologies that have not yet been invented to solve problems that we do not even know are problems yet. A school system that does not teach students the skills required for being emotionally and socially competent and to have strong communication, technological, and life skills will leave them without the skills they need to succeed in the workforce.

Technological advances now allow work to be carved up and shipped around the world. American workers are now competing and collaborating with workers from all parts of the world. Therefore, a school system that does not teach students the skills for collaborating in diverse environments nor provide them with knowledge, skills, and understandings of world languages, geography, history, religion, and culture will put them at a disadvantage in a global economy.

Lastly, individuals now shoulder increased responsibility for managing their own well-being. For example, fewer defined-benefits plans exist, and consumers are increasingly being called upon to choose health care coverage and care. In addition, employment is now more contingent on performance than loyalty. A school system that does not prepare individuals to make health, civic, and financial decisions and to live a physically and mentally healthy life will leave them unprepared to make decisions that will become increasingly important.

Some of these changes, like the Common Core Curriculum Standards and new teacher evaluation requirements, may have been mandated. Other changes, like increased use of personal devices in classrooms, are local decisions. Minor, technical changes are usually tolerated without much resistance. However, regardless of the source of the change, major changes to the status quo have significant consequences for superintendents.

Even change that makes sense or is mandated from an outside source is dangerous. Because habits provide a feeling of stability, change results in a loss of predictability. In short, for most educators, the status quo is pleasant, whereas improvement is a pain in the ass.

For many teachers, the changes articulated in our grading policy were new. In the beginning, they did not know how these changes would impact this aspect of their job. In general, people do not like and will seek to resolve uncertainty. They may claim to want change, and they do but only if the change requires minimal sacrifice on their part.

In addition, change challenges a person's sense of competence. Habits, values, and attitudes, even dysfunctional ones, are part of one's identity (Heifetz and Linsky 2002). For some teachers, changing how they grade student work required changing how they defined themselves as a teacher. With new grading practices that focus on grades as a more accurate tool of communicating student progress, some teachers had to give up the use of grades as a tool for punishment and control.

IMPACT ON SUPERINTENDENTS

The distress resulting from uncertainty and loss of identity can be severe. Severe distress can make people act cruel (Heifetz 1994). Empathy, compassion, and mental flexibility are sacrificed to the desperate need for order. Those who feel they have gotten or might be on the receiving end of negative outcomes resulting from a change will attempt to resist.

One part of this resistance will be an expression of hostility to the perceived source of the change. Fair or not, leaders come to represent the loss associated with any substantial change to a school system (Coda and Jetter 2016). The implicit and sometimes explicit operating principle is that, if we can weaken the leader, then we can preserve what we have. If we can weaken the leader, we can submerge the attempted change, and order will be restored. Therefore, while change is both necessary and inevitable, those who lead during these changes will be attacked.

Personal attacks are a tried-and-true method of neutralizing change. Whatever form the attack takes, if it is successful, then the subject of the conversation is turned from the content of the change being advanced to the character or style of the person leading the change. With attention focused on subjects like the leader's style or personality, the issue gets submerged.

Yet, ironically, a superintendent's personality or style will rarely be criticized when they are delivering good news. In general, people make criticism personal only when they do not like the message. Thus, rather than focusing on the content of the message, the opponents of a change will frequently find it more effective to discredit the leader.

The attacks will go after your character, competence, motives, and even your personal life. Your views will likely be distorted and misrepresented. The attacks will come in whatever form your opponents' think will work. They will come at you wherever they can find a vulnerability. However, even if there are merits to these criticisms, the blame is largely misplaced. If the change is mandated or necessary, the content and subject of that change still remain.

When this occurs, a superintendent must recognize this effort for what it is. It is an attempt to divert attention from an issue that is troubling to people.

Superintendents cannot allow themselves to become the issue. They must respond to these attacks in ways that place the focus back where it should be, on the substance of the change.

It is difficult to remain focused on the issue when you are being attacked. However, when you take attacks personally, you are conspiring with those who seek to derail your efforts. Usually, how you manage these attacks is more important than the substance of the accusations. It is at times like these that superintendents must remember that those we lead don't love or hate us. In fact, they probably don't even know you well. They love or hate the changes you have come to represent.

Another time-honored way to derail change efforts is diversion (Heifetz and Linsky 2002). There are many ways in which staff and community will try to make leaders lose focus. They may attempt to broaden the agenda to include unrelated issues or overwhelm the superintendent with requests. For example, they may claim that, to implement these changes, unattainable and unrelated resources are required.

In the grading situation described previously, resistant staff members claimed they could not provide retakes without compensation for time to administer them either before or after school. We did not have the funds to do this, nor was it necessary. As had been done voluntarily by many teachers in the past, these retakes could be offered in class. Negative teacher leaders were attempting to insert a barrier into the change process in an effort to thwart the overall grading policy changes.

Another example is stating that the changes cannot be implemented without first making other unrelated changes to other aspects of the system. Once again, resistant staff members attempted to derail changes to the grading policy by claiming that first we needed to change the student code of conduct. It was posited that students would not be motivated to put forth their best effort unless we included negative consequences for specific behaviors in our student code of conduct. This was an attempt to divert the issue from providing clearer feedback related to student performance to student discipline.

It is easy to become diverted by other people's demands, but a superintendent cannot allow themselves to lose focus on what needs to be accomplished. The superintendent must see these diversions for what they are and counteract them effectively. The future of their school system likely depends on it.

SOLUTIONS

There are many well-researched suggestions for leading and managing change efforts. Successful implementation of change requires that we acknowledge the loss being experienced, provide a preferred vision for the future with valid rationale, model appropriate behavior, manage the pace of the work, and work collaboratively with those impacted by the changes.

Collaborative decision-making can be important. Yet some teachers find it much easier to let administrators make all the decisions and do all the work. Then, they can grumble about the outcomes and complain that they were not consulted in making the decision.

Other teachers will seize the opportunity to exercise influence on decisions that impact their daily responsibilities. An effective, representative teacher work group can result in outcomes that have an improved probability of success. However, this requires selecting the right teachers to do an appropriate, clearly defined task. Group composition is too important to be left to chance.

Additionally, the task must focus on a topic such as curriculum, instruction, assessment, or student code of conduct. These types of tasks are meaningful to faculty because they impact their daily lives. Tasks that appear more administrative in nature will be viewed by teachers as your requiring them to do your job for you.

Regardless of how well one leads these changes, the leader will be held responsible for the disequilibrium generated by the process, the losses people had to absorb, and the backlash resulting from those who felt left behind. As a result, even change efforts that have positive results will likely have a negative impact on the length and quality of your tenure.

In this chapter, the case has been made that change is both necessary and inevitable. Because the nature of change is difficult and uncomfortable, it is likely to be resisted. Resistance often comes through personal attacks and diversions meant to shift attention.

If we are to be successful agents of change in our school districts, superintendents must be aware of and use strategies to effectively counteract these efforts. Counteracting efforts to shift attention requires tremendous self-discipline and perseverance. However, even with effective change leadership and management strategies, negative feelings will result.

Because these lingering negative feelings will very likely be attributed to those in charge, others will seek revenge. Eventually, even the best change leaders will encounter efforts to silence them. This is especially true for those with the most to lose from your successful implementation of the changes.

CONCLUSION

Change leadership is a major responsibility of an effective superintendent. If you choose to become the leader of a school district, you have the responsibility to make the changes necessary to improve the quality of education children receive. Be aware that, instead of receiving applause for your efforts, you will be criticized. You must have the capacity to stomach this hostility.

In the end, even though it will likely shorten your tenure in one place, you will be able to sleep well at night knowing that you improved the quality of a school system because you believed that children deserved better. The best leaders derive an intrinsic satisfaction from doing the right work in the right way. Doing the right work in the right way can be difficult with teachers and community members. These are the subjects of our next two chapters.

KEY POINTS OF THIS CHAPTER

- For most educators, the status quo is pleasant, whereas improvement is a pain in the ass.
- Fair or not, leaders come to represent the loss and uncertainty associated with major changes to the status quo.
- There will be an effort to undermine or weaken the leader of any significant change effort.
- Regardless of how well one leads these changes, the leader will be held responsible for the disequilibrium generated by the process, the losses people had to absorb, and the backlash resulting from those who felt left behind.

QUESTIONS FOR DISCUSSION OR REFLECTION

1. Is it a moral and professional imperative for a superintendent to be a change leader? Is it worth the risk to your career and the hostility it may provoke?
2. How can you manage and lead the changes you seek to make to minimize the personal damage and attain the desired results?

Truth Three

In General, Teachers Are a Difficult Group to Lead

> Working with kids is easy; working with adults is hard. Working with adversarial adults is even harder, and working with irrational, blood-thirsty, revengeful adults is unbearable.
>
> —Coda and Jetter

In about my fourth year as a superintendent, my administrative team and I were struggling with the fact that, despite all our efforts to provide our staff with additional curriculum materials, professional development opportunities, planning time, and technology, there was still a general sense of negativity. We could never seem to give enough, and that was consistently being used as the reason for a lack of results.

Thus, we came up with the brilliant idea to send staff members to other districts to observe and interact with their teachers. The thought was that, if they saw the conditions of teachers in other districts, they would experience an increased sense of appreciation for what they had. The lack of things could not be used as an excuse if people with less were achieving the same or better results.

We arranged the visits with local districts and provided substitute coverage. All we asked for in return was a written report summarizing the visit. When we received those reports, all they contained was a list of everything those teachers had that our teachers didn't. Instead of appreciating their own good fortune, the teachers found a way to further express disappointment with what they did not have.

Another time, I decided that I would host a staff luncheon for teacher appreciation. I used personal expenses to pay for all of the food and supplies. I stayed late into the evening to decorate the faculty room in each school building. My wife drove with our children to deliver the food before lunchtime.

I hoped that an effort such as this would let the staff know that I appreciated them for the hard work they were doing on behalf of the children. Instead of recognizing this gesture as a sign of appreciation, I received complaints that we ran out of cookies before everyone could get one and there was no milk provided for the coffee.

In fact, staff members actually compared what was provided at each school building to make sure it was equitably distributed. My secretary was contacted to see if she would redistribute the leftovers at each building so that there would be enough for everyone the next day. Experiences such as these have led me to conclude that, as a group, teachers can be a challenge to lead.

CHALLENGES OF LEADING TEACHERS

I have great respect and admiration for many of the teachers I have worked with and supervised over the years. Most of them, even those who were marginally effective, cared about their students. Many of them worked hard in the face of difficult circumstances. I respect the profession and most of the people who choose it as a vocation.

Without a doubt, teaching is a stressful job. If it is to be done well, it requires high levels of knowledge and skill combined with abundant mental and physical stamina. It deserves more respect and recognition than it receives. It is a noble profession with incredible responsibility for the future of our society. Yet it is not right for everyone.

Teaching is unique when compared to other professions. Almost all of the work teachers do is outside the view of their supervisors. Teachers can write lesson plans, and administrators can review them. But it is not possible to know if they are actually following those plans. Teachers can receive professional development, but usually no one has the resources to ensure they are applying what they have learned.

Holding people accountable for daily performance is a leap of faith. We must trust that our teaches are doing the right things, in the right way. We must trust that they are providing high-quality instruction of the defined school curriculum. Fortunately, many but not all of them do.

Teachers are able to earn tenure. While there are valid reasons for tenure, it should never be used as a shield to hide poor performance and low productivity. The best form of tenure is competent performance.

Yet, in countless situations, superintendents must accept and try to work to improve the performance and productivity of teachers who have greater job security than they do. It is very difficult to be held accountable for achieving results when staff believe they can simply wait you out. With the churn at the top in so many school districts, they may correctly conclude they will simply outlast you.

Teachers spend the majority of their day working with children. They can be great with kids in a classroom but have very little skill for working with adults, especially those who are in positions of authority (Black and English 2001). Some teachers are just awful with adults. They can be great in the classroom and have terrible relationships with colleagues and adversarial relationships with administrators. Yet these teachers often become beloved by parents and are viewed as great teachers.

Based on the impression parents receive from their children, they draw conclusions about the quality of a teacher. Parents and community members do not understand or in most cases even care that a school is a system. A strong system requires that teachers do more than work within the four walls of their classroom.

Teachers must work collaboratively with colleagues and administrators to create common curriculum and assessments. They must work on standing and ad hoc committees to address specific tasks and issues. They must attend meetings and express their thoughts and opinions appropriately. The level of collegiality and professionalism of each teaching staff member has a major impact on the overall culture and climate of the school. Yet, heaven forbid, a supposed "great" teacher be held accountable for poor adult behavior. The community will form a posse that will seek to ride the responsible administrator out of town.

In general, teachers are highly sensitive about status differentials. This became painfully obvious to me when one novice teacher shared with me her experience of being chastised in the staff room for taking the seat of a veteran staff member at a lunch table. Unbeknownst to me, and apparently this teacher, novice teachers were expected to earn the right through longevity to sit with the veteran teachers. Teachers often equate length of longevity with level of status.

Those who have been in the school system longer believe they should receive preferential treatment. This expectation is regardless of performance or ability. In my case, asking a very knowledgeable and highly skilled non-tenured teacher to complete curriculum work was considered an insult to veteran staff members. Her repeatedly demonstrated knowledge and skills did not matter. Vocal veteran staff members expressed their opinion that she had not earned the right to do this work because she had not been in the school system long enough.

Longevity can be important for developing wisdom through experience. However, if a teacher has one year of experience repeated twenty times, then longevity does not equate to much. It is not the length of time a teacher is in a position that determines their knowledge and skill. It is the quality of that time that matters.

Younger teachers are sometimes bullied by veteran teachers to stay in line. If they work too hard or innovate too much, they may be accused of trying to make other teachers look bad. These behaviors, which an administrator may not even be aware of, are antithetical to creating positive and productive school cultures. In fact, teachers with less experience are often uncomfortable or unwilling to share their good ideas for fear of the negative perceptions of others.

Teachers are highly sensitive to criticism (Black and English 2001). Yet it is the job of the administrator to evaluate and seek to improve teacher performance. No matter how nice we try to be or how strategic we are with providing this feedback, it is often met with predictable behaviors. One of these behaviors is to shift blame to others for the situation or behavior. It is the students, parents, other teachers, or your fault for their actions. I could do what you want me to only if . . .

Another predictable behavior is to justify behavior based on the expectations of a previous supervisor. Comments describing how the previous superintendent or principal was alright with a specific behavior are meant to undermine confidence and make the current administrator back down on their demands.

Rarely have I met with a teacher who took ownership for poor behavior or low productivity. Instead, regardless of how you deliver the message, they take it as a personal affront and are not shy about sharing that opinion with others.

IMPACT ON SUPERINTENDENTS

The fact is that you are everyone's friend until you start telling the truth. When you tell teachers they are not perfect, many of them can't take that reality. And when you tell them they can't do something they want to do, no matter what the reason is, many teachers will become insulted or angered. They will express these emotions to other teachers. Sometimes, they will use community connections and relationships to secretly drum up personal support.

It is important to remember that many teachers have little to no awareness of the effectiveness of their peers' teaching abilities. They feel that, if someone is nice to them, they are probably a good teacher. If they work with someone who has shown them personal concern in times of need, then they assume these are people who are also likely to be good with children.

Thus, when a teacher shares their gripes with colleagues, it is often met with sympathy or concern that they will be the next victim. Even when you are aware of a teacher sharing this type of information with colleagues, there is little you can do to change the narrative because it is a personnel matter subject to confidentiality on the part of the administrator.

Despite all of the advances in instrumentation and practice for teacher evaluation, I have come up with one simple question I use to gauge teacher performance. Would I want my own child in this classroom? If the answer is no, then I have no right putting other parents' children in that class. In this situation, it is my moral and ethical responsibility to do whatever is necessary to increase this teacher's effectiveness or remove that teacher. Of course, this must be done professionally and appropriately, regardless of how others act.

Some staff members will actually be relieved and may even secretly admire you for taking action to remove an incompetent teacher. This is especially true if that teacher's negative performance had any impact on completion of their own job responsibilities. However, they will never publicly admit it. That would go against the norms of the profession.

Hold enough people accountable, and you will create staff resentment and unrest. One weapon staff will use to respond to your attempts to hold them accountable or improve their performance is to claim that morale is bad. Morale is important, but it is not the sole responsibility of the administration. As a state of mind, morale is a choice. We each can choose to be proud of the fact that we work in a district that has high standards for staff and student performance, or we can choose to play the role of the victim.

Regardless, claims about morale are very strong weapons the community will respond to. It is ironic that, by holding teachers accountable to improve performance and productivity for the district's children, you will create community concern that teachers are unhappy. The message is to provide my child with a top-notch education, but do not create the discomfort necessary to spur growth among the staff.

A superintendent must always treat all staff members with dignity and respect. All staff deserve leadership that includes integrity, honesty, and appropriate support. Yet, as leaders, we must not avoid doing and saying what must be done simply to keep others happy. It may be the safe approach, but it is cowardly.

Teachers are often suspicious of the motivations of those in authority. Perhaps because they have never done the job of the superintendent, they often assume negative motivations behind actions and decisions. I have had teachers repeatedly express to others that decisions were made or actions were taken because of nefarious reasons.

For example, I have been accused of rigging where parking spaces are assigned by principals in order to get back at specific staff members. Additionally, teachers have expressed suspicion that I made sure they were assigned lunch duty so it would force them to seek retirement. In both cases, neither did I have any involvement in either decision, nor did I have any investment in the outcomes of those decisions.

The point is not the ludicrous nature of these examples; rather, it is the paranoia that some staff members demonstrate. It has been surprising to me that, without any evidence for or history of malicious behavior, teachers will assume you don't like them or you are out to get them.

A superintendent does owe a proper explanation to a staff member when a decision is made or an action is taken that has potentially serious consequences related to their job responsibilities. This explanation may be provided by their immediate supervisor or the superintendent themself. However, we simply do not have the time to explain every action or decision to staff. In the absence of this information or even despite it, teachers frequently explain leadership behavior through the lens of paranoia.

A quality school system depends on having a quality staff. More than most industries, education is labor intensive. In fact, 70 to 80 percent of most school budgets are dedicated to people.

The most effective school systems manage to promote synergy by getting individuals to work as a team. More than simply the sum of each faculty member, the faculty as a whole combine to produce more than they could have accomplished individually. To achieve this effect, it helps to understand the types of faculty members who compose each school district.

The first type of faculty member found in a school district is the "franchise player." These are the hardest working, most talented staff members. They expect to have autonomy in order to do what they believe is best for their students. They love teaching and are motivated to achieve greatness in their classrooms. They often put in long hours dedicated to improving their craft and seek out their own professional development opportunities. They do not want to be overly constrained by administration or unions. These are the superstars of every school district. However, because they are iconoclasts, other faculty members and sometimes principals may resent them or have difficulty working with them.

However, most teachers are not franchise players. Most teachers are "backbones." Usually the largest percentage of the faculty, these teachers are average to slightly above average. They will work hard and are dedicated to the success of their students. They are good colleagues, willing and able to engage in collegial efforts.

A significant difference between superstars and backbones is that backbone faculty members need regular affirmation of their efforts from others. Whereas superstars do the work for intrinsic satisfaction, the backbones need external affirmation to keep putting forth high effort levels. Even if grudgingly done, backbones will comply with administrative requests and are usually also compliant, but not zealous, union members.

The final category of employee is the "sloth." These are the masters of mediocrity. Sloths "work" only in school. They put in their time and little else. They complain frequently and are interested first and foremost in security and stability. These are the resident members of the bitching and sniping section of the faculty room. Sloths are whiners who want to do the absolute minimum required to continue earning a paycheck. The only time you will see a sloth put forward a great deal of effort is when it comes to union activities designed to protect them. Obviously, the fewer sloths the school district has, the better the overall quality of a faculty will be.

The superintendent must know what category each of their faculty members falls into and then treat them accordingly. A franchise player needs autonomy, but they also must understand the outer limits that define their work. For example, they cannot simply discard the district curriculum because they don't agree with it. They are a part of a system, but within that system they need freedom to be innovative. They are often bored by whole-faculty staff development opportunities.

Backbones need a lot of attention and support. They need positive strokes on a regular basis. Frequently, because they are good team players, backbones are a good fit for district-level committee work. In addition, backbones tend to embrace and at least partially apply content shared during district staff development opportunities.

Sloths need to get better, or they need to get out of education. A faculty member may have always been a sloth, or they have developed into one. Perhaps time has passed them by, and they have not kept up or have become jaded due to experience. Regardless of the reason, every child in an incompetent teacher's class is losing one-twelfth of their entire public school education. That is not acceptable.

Sloths do not engage in or apply information presented in district staff development opportunities. They will not get better unless there are significant negative personal ramifications for not doing so. At best, they hide during these professional development sessions so they are not noticed. At worst, they are argumentative and disrespectful to those providing the content.

Yet medals are not awarded for the dirty work that it sometimes takes to ensure competence in classrooms. There is not a bad teacher who wasn't loved by some kid or parent somewhere. Be prepared to pay the price.

As a result of your dedication to first-rate teaching, unions may despise you, and some teachers will fear you. Expect to be vilified, not appreciated for demanding high-quality teaching in every classroom. If you are the kind of person who needs public accolades, libraries named in your honor, or scholarships given in your memory, the superintendent job may not be for you.

Three types of school employees besides faculty deserve special attention. First, is the superintendent's secretary. I have had the fortune of working with many great secretaries over the years and some not so great. I have learned that a good secretary is vital to the success of the superintendent. Secretaries are the cryptographers of the school system. Often, they know things no one else does. If they trust you and have your best interest in mind, they will make sure you are aware of information you need to know.

In addition, they are the first line of defense against others' attempts to create problems for you. A secretary who believes they are valued will stick their neck out when necessary to protect you. Additionally, the first impression that others will have of you is often drawn from your secretary. Whether it be how they handle a phone call or greet visitors, they will send a message to everyone about how your office is managed. Everyone who reads your secretary's body language will know what type of mood you are in on that day.

No one can make or break the superintendent like their secretary. It is wise to remember the importance of this relationship. When working with your secretary, always remember these two things. First, secretaries do professional work, and domestics do chores. Do not degrade their professionalism by expecting them to do tasks unrelated to their job responsibilities. Second, Administrative Assistants Day is one of the most important holidays on the school calendar! Treat it as such.

Another source of information and importance is building head custodians. The best head custodians maintain their school like it was their own home. They make sure classrooms are always spotless. In addition, they often get to know the kids and the teachers. At a basic level, people will assume that, if you can't keep the schools clean, then there is little chance you will be able to improve learning. The real basics are always custodial, so you need head custodians who are effective.

Finally, there are the school nurses. I have had the good fortune of working with many highly competent nurses over the course of my career. While they can have tunnel vision on specific issues and can be pushy with their demands, they have always demonstrated a commitment to the health of students as well as the school as a whole. Because of the nature of their work, they know more about the students and their families than anyone else in the district. The nurse can be a tremendous source of information for helping make sense of delicate situations.

This chapter would be incomplete without discussion of local teacher unions. On the one hand, over the years, I have been blessed to work with teacher union leaders who were very effective. While representing their members appropriately and professionally, behind the scenes they held their members to high standards. These individuals set the tone for their membership that teaching was a profession.

On the other hand, I have worked with local teacher union leaders who were petty and vindictive. They used their power to file ridiculous grievances on items like all of the district's clocks not being synchronized to the minute and not receiving compensation for members who remained a few minutes late for bus duty due to bad weather.

Local teacher unions serve a purpose. They bargain for appropriate working conditions and compensation. Additionally, they work to ensure that provisions in the collective bargaining agreement are adhered to. Agree with them or not, it is the superintendent's responsibility to abide by contractual agreements.

Local teacher unions are not the enemy of the administration. They can be valuable partners. However, that depends on the composition of the local leadership team. True faculty leaders who understand the requirements of being professionals are very valuable to a school system. Union hacks who want to be treated like professionals yet advocate for doing nothing extra unless they are paid for it are cancerous to a school system.

In general, a superintendent has to learn to work with those the staff has selected as local union leadership. To do otherwise is to risk inappropriately interfering with the internal activities of the union. Getting involved in the internal activities of local union leadership risks violating federal and state labor laws and will ultimately result in lost grievances.

CONCLUSION

Teaching is a noble profession. Schools are only as good as the quality of teachers in them. That is why every hiring opportunity must be treated as a gift and every effective teacher must be valued. Likewise, every ineffective teacher must either significantly improve or be dismissed.

Yet some unique features of the profession make it difficult to lead teachers effectively. Many teachers are highly sensitive to status differentials, are suspicious of authority, and resist change. Frequently, teachers are easily insulted, provoked, or angered. In general, they are used to dealing with students and often have a difficult time working with other adults, especially those in authority. Whereas teachers need coursework in child psychology, administrators often benefit from coursework in abnormal psychology.

Most of a teacher's work is done without direct supervision. In addition, they have lifetime tenure, and the superintendent does not. Oftentimes, due to the length of this tenure, they have community connections and relationships they will use to drum up support for opposition. If a superintendent pushes too hard or fast, they will likely be told they are lowering staff morale. With claims about morale issues, the superintendent and not the staff will receive the blame.

A successful superintendent learns to navigate these issues. Leadership requires that the superintendent do what is right and necessary. Yet it must be done strategically, appropriately, and professionally. If actions are taken in this manner, they may earn respect, but they will not earn popularity. A superintendent must be OK with not being liked. Respect as a professional must be the ultimate goal. Another group for whom this must be the case is the community. This is the subject of the next chapter.

KEY POINTS OF THIS CHAPTER

- The vast majority of a teacher's work is done without supervision.
- It is very difficult to be held accountable for achieving results when staff believe they can simply wait you out.
- Some teachers are just awful with other adults.
- Teachers often equate longer longevity with higher status.
- You will be everyone's friend until you start telling the truth.
- When assessing teacher performance, ask yourself if you would want your own child in this classroom? If the answer is no, then you have no right putting other parents' children in that class.
- Parents and community members want it both ways. They want you to provide their children with a top-notch education, but they do not want you to create the discomfort necessary to spur growth among the staff.
- In the absence of information or even despite it, teachers frequently explain leadership behavior through the lens of paranoia.

QUESTIONS FOR DISCUSSION OR REFLECTION

1. Do you agree with the goal of earning respect, instead of seeking popularity? Are you willing to make respect for your professionalism the ultimate goal of your actions?
2. How will you respond to the claims of low staff morale?
3. Which of your faculty members are "franchise players," "backbones," and "sloths"? What is your plan for increasing the number of franchise players and backbones while decreasing the number of sloths?
4. How will you manage teachers who use personal relationship and community connections to undermine your efforts?

Truth Four

There Is No Such Thing as the "Community"

The community is a mirage.

—Black and English

In my ninth year as a superintendent, I was considering moving on to another school district. I was a finalist for a position and had been told that I was very likely to be offered the job. Around this time, as a surprise to me, my current district's school business administrator informed me and the board that he had accepted a new position. Because of the nature of the relationship I had created with this composition of the board, they knew that I was actively exploring other opportunities. Upon receiving word that the business administrator was leaving, they asked me to consider renewal of my contract to stay with the district.

We engaged in negotiations, and, admittedly, I was eventually offered a generous contract. I withdrew from my other searches. Upon word that my contract was going to be renewed, a small but vocal group in the community began to voice their objections. Through social media and other forms of communication, they distorted and misused information to get others to join them in resisting this contract renewal.

Soon, everyone who perceived that I had aggrieved them in some manner in the past was joining in bashing me personally and professionally. Others who did not even know me or had never met me joined in as well. While still a small minority of the population of the community, it became a vocal minority.

It came time for the meeting for the board to vote on this contract. Approximately a hundred people were in the crowd. This was a large group for one of our board of education meetings. Some were there as curious observers, while others were there to draw blood. When it came time for public comment, the critics made outrageous, false comments about me both personally and professionally. Of course, as was standard practice, the board listened to the input but did not respond. Eventually, the board unanimously approved the new contract.

During the course of this experience and afterward, I received many private statements of support. However, none of these people wanted to engage with the critics on Facebook or in public meetings for fear of becoming the next target. This experience taught me three things. One, the loudest voices do not necessarily represent the majority. Two, for some there is no such thing as institutional loyalty. Three, when you are a semipublic figure, you are fair game for all types of criticism. You develop adversaries, and they may not fight fair in an effort to get their way.

CHALLENGES OF THE COMMUNITY

When the term *community* is used by educators and board members, it is often used incorrectly. Rarely does the community act as a single entity. Rather, it reacts to events. The community rarely speaks with one voice. There are many voices. It is rarely true when someone states that everyone feels the same way about an issue as they do. The silent majority does exist.

Most community members demonstrate apathy about their schools unless a specific issue prompts them to have a strong emotional reaction. A small percentage of community members actually vote in school board elections, and an even smaller percentage attend or are aware of what occurs at school board meetings. Community surveys and focus groups do not have a high participation rate. Thus, unfortunately it is hard to determine what a community wants from either elections or official public comments.

This does not mean that a small, vociferous minority cannot sound like a majority. These groups use social media and other opportunities to act as if they represent everyone. A wise superintendent and board of education must be able to keep their statements in perspective.

Every community has factions with different interests and priorities. Almost everyone in a community would agree they want students to receive a high-quality education in a fiscally responsible manner. However, what defines a high-quality education and fiscal responsibility varies widely among community members.

To some groups, high-quality education focuses on excellence in the arts. Other groups want the return to basics with a heavy emphasis on grammar and spelling. Some groups believe that excellence in athletics must be the goal, while others believe that this should not be the responsibility of the school district. Frequently, for municipal officials and senior citizens on fixed incomes, fiscal responsibility has a very different meaning than it does to parents of school-age children.

When varying expectations are combined with limited resources, the result is competing interests. Thus, conflicting expectations, needs and wants, and multiple agendas are inevitable. This is often painfully evident during the budget development process. If there is a need to make difficult budget decisions that impact the allocation of resources, someone has to lose. A decision needs to be made that will disappoint someone. At these times, the leaders will receive the greatest share of the criticism (Polka and Litchka 2008).

The groups that tend to lose the least are those that are the best organized and therefore the most vocal. Groups of people with similar interests, for example, band parents or sports boosters, can attract similar people. By growing their numbers, these groups gain power and justify their behavior. There is power in numbers, even if those who are counted in those numbers are irrational, blind followers to people with hidden motives (Spencer 2013). Importantly, even with increased numbers these groups rarely represent the majority.

IMPACT ON SUPERINTENDENTS

It is not uncommon for superintendents to encounter attempted political manipulations as they make decisions for the good of the school system. I have experienced both veiled and explicit threats from local elected officials and representatives of township programs as they attempted to secure specific action on behalf of the groups they represent.

As a result of being stuck between competing interests, superintendents and boards often proceed cautiously. The necessary decisions are made in a way that is designed not to offend specific interest groups. Unfortunately, these compromises result in half measures that do not adequately address the needs of those who have no voice, the students. Compromise done in the best interests of our students is necessary and unavoidable. Compromise intended to only meet the needs of adults is unacceptable.

Should we really cut a literacy coach position to order new uniforms for the school football and basketball teams? Should we cut professional development for staff so that we can retain an additional music teacher we don't need for anything but concert band? Sometimes, it takes courage and a willingness to risk your position to do what is right for a school system. Politics in particular have been singled out as a primary reason superintendents are fired from or choose to leave their position (Melton et al. 2019).

Without a doubt, a superintendent who tells people what they need to hear rather than what they want to hear risks people's ire and increases the superintendent's vulnerability. Exercising leadership with integrity can get you in a lot of trouble. Telling a parent that their child made a poor behavioral choice that will result in consequences that can result in a new adversary.

Refusing to change a valid grade assignment because of a parent's request can make you enemies. Calling Child Protective Services because of suspected neglect or abuse can result in someone who will want revenge. Regardless of the misplaced blame, little by little with each unpopular decision you make you are expending finite political capital.

Despite being hardworking, well educated, and highly motivated to do the job required, if you fulfill your role with integrity, you will eventually make decisions that someone or some group doesn't like. Done enough times, you will become the target in the community. At this time, you will discover that, when it comes to the rules of war, there are none.

Fortunately, the attacks are rarely physical. The primary tool that adversaries employ is misuse of information. Rather than focus on the content of your message, taking issue with its merits, adversaries find it more effective to discredit you. One result is that all too commonly rumors are spread about the superintendent. These rumors may take the form of telling others that the superintendent is having an affair with a staff member or has mental or physical health issues. They may claim the superintendent is financially corrupt or is taking advantage of the system for personal gain.

If any of these things are true, they are very serious concerns. However, when these career-bashing rumors are created and spread without any basis, they are very hurtful and harmful. This is especially true when they are amplified by print or social media.

With all of its potential benefits, the internet's ability to spread information quickly and anonymously is a challenge for school leaders. This is particularly true with adversaries who create false or damaging information for their victims. Anonymous online postings in which nasty shots are taken are to be expected. The digital traces of these attacks do not go away and can become career crippling. Yet, as semipublic figures, superintendents have a very difficult time proving slander.

In addition, it is wise to never get in a fight with a skunk because even if you win you will come out smelling bad. You will not win these types of contests because it is very likely that you will not be willing to sink to the depths your opponents are willing to go.

The emotions of your adversaries will drive them to obsess upon their desire to bring you down. Their deeply rooted belief system will lead them to justify the harm they inflict. Even if you do sink to those depths, you will not be demonstrating what the rest of the community expects of leaders. Being equally toxic will only lead more people to believe your adversaries are correct about you.

Since it is counterproductive for you to engage in your own self-defense, when public attacks are launched, you would hope that supporters would come to your defense. Yet, most of the time, the superintendent will be left asking where was everyone when they went through this? You will receive private messages of support, and some may even admire your reactions. Few, if any, want to risk taking a public stance out of fear that they will become the next target. A superintendent will never feel more alone than when they are under heavy attack by merciless adversaries.

Another misuse of information is Open Public Records Act requests. These can serve a legitimate purpose, but they can also be abused. Adversaries can use abundant requests for information as a tool to clog the system. These fishing expeditions do not serve any legitimate purpose, except to harass the personnel in the school system.

Sometimes, adversaries will use litigation just to damage you. They can make false claims to state education officials or the board of education. Even when baseless, these claims require the expense of legal fees and the time involved with investigations. Even when you are cleared of any wrongdoing, the cloud of suspicion follows you. Often, as will be discussed in truth 9, the news media do not sell the truth; they use sensationalism to sell newspapers. Even when the content of the article has facts that establish innocence, the headlines are usually provocative.

Most superintendents would agree that it does not hurt that much when people question decisions or criticize actions. You get used to the fact that many people believe they can do better what you have been trained to do. Ultimately, debating ideas is healthy and can lead to better outcomes. However, it can be tremendously hurtful when personal attacks question your character and integrity. The result can be a loss in the belief that the world is fair, ethical, and just. Eventually cynicism can creep into your soul.

Over time, some superintendents use cynicism to cover up their wounded ideals (Dotlich, Noel, and Walker 2004). As a result, they become leaders who work without purpose. They may do their jobs efficiently and effectively, but they do so without any real sense of commitment. The phrase "it is just a job" becomes the mantra.

Another reaction is to assume the role of the victim. Self-pity is neither pretty, nor is it productive. Whether you play the role of the victim is a choice. If you choose to lead, then you must do so with energy and passion. You must remain willing to go the extra mile and take risks that put you on the edge. Our schools and the future of our children depend on having passionate and purposeful leaders.

Some superintendents believe themselves to be at fault. They believe that working harder is the recourse for trying to make things right. Be assured that working harder and spending yourself physically and emotionally to do the job will not stop most adversaries. It is when a superintendent is under attack that they need to maintain the structures in their life that keep them healthy. This is not the time to sacrifice time at the gym or with loved ones. This is the time when those activities are needed more than ever.

SOLUTIONS

So how do you handle these attacks? Assuming that we have no control over society gaining a heightened sense of decency and civility, we can control only our own responses. One way to successfully cope with these attacks is by depersonalizing them. It is helpful to remember that, when you lead people, they don't love or hate you. Mostly, they don't even know you. They love or hate the positions you represent.

Adversaries' deeply rooted negative attitudes are often the result of experiences that left them feeling victimized in some way (Coda and Jetter 2016). Their hurtful or spiteful behavior is often a response to or the result of such experiences and usually has very little if anything to do with you personally. Realizing that their behavior is about them and how they react to the world allows you to depersonalize their merciless attacks and empowers you to respond objectively.

With emotional objectivity, you can remain cool when the world around you is boiling. The people who challenge you are testing your steadiness and will judge your response to their attacks. Usually, it is your management of the attack more than the substance that will determine your fate. At best, your adversaries may gain a newfound respect for your calmness in handling the situation; at worst, you do not give them the satisfaction of getting the response they want to elicit. An emotionally charged response may feel good, but it will be of little value.

CONCLUSION

The community is not a single entity. It consists of factions with competing interests. Each faction has its own wants and needs. In a situation that requires difficult decisions due to limited resources, eventually someone will be disappointed. This group will not be happy that their agenda was selected as the one required to make sacrifices. Another group of people that will not be happy are those parents and community members to whom you told bad news. Telling the truth as you see it may lead to resentment and in some cases the quest for revenge.

Every superintendent, some sooner, some later, comes to the frightening conclusion from firsthand experience that life is not fair and that some people swept up in their own agendas can be very cruel. Of course, all of this can be avoided or at least forestalled if the superintendent always takes the path of least resistance, making inappropriate compromises and telling everyone what they want to hear. This may increase career longevity, but it is not the leadership our schools need.

Some adversaries will go to great lengths to damage you. Those who seek to damage you will use whatever vehicles they can to attack your character or competence. They will distort and misrepresent your views. They will harass you mercilessly.

As a result, some superintendents become cynical, and others allow themselves to feel victimized. Still others try to work harder, sacrificing the very stability and structures needed when feeling alone and vulnerable. Understandable but counterproductive reactions. The only thing you can control is how you respond to your adversary's efforts. Depersonalizing the attacks makes it possible to respond with emotional objectivity. In the long run, how you respond is usually more important than the substance of the attack itself. We turn now to those who are elected to represent the community, the board of education.

KEY POINTS OF THIS CHAPTER

- Most community members demonstrate apathy about their schools, unless a specific issue prompts them to have a strong emotional reaction.
- Every community consists of different factions. Each faction has its own interests and priorities.
- The combination of competing priorities with limited resources leads to conflict.
- Compromise done in the best interests of our students is necessary and unavoidable.
- Compromise intended to meet only the needs of adults is unacceptable.
- For some community members and groups, when it comes to the rules of war, there are none.
- Never get in a fight with a skunk; even if you win, you will come out smelling bad.
- When you lead people, they don't love or hate you. Mostly, they don't even know you. They love or hate the positions you represent.
- Usually, it is your management of the attack and not the substance that will determine your fate.

QUESTIONS FOR DISCUSSION OR REFLECTION

1. Who are the major factions in the community you serve? What do they want?

2. What will you do when limited resources force you to make a decision that has a negative impact on one of these factions?
3. How will you respond when you develop adversaries because you tell the truth as you see it?
4. How will you handle it when adversaries unfairly attack your character or competence and distort or misrepresent your views?

Truth Five

Your "Boss" Is Not Qualified to Do Their Job

> Someone you would not trust to care for your family pet can win a school board election.
>
> —Spencer

As the night progressed past eleven o'clock and board members were still engaged in debate about district snow plowing contracts, I once again began to question the effectiveness of board meetings. Board members had spent almost an hour on this topic, it was getting late, and ironically it was beginning to snow. Yet we rarely if ever spent this same amount of time on the topics of curriculum, instruction, or assessment.

As I pondered this situation, a realization hit me. They all could relate to and understand snow plowing, but, because of their backgrounds, the only thing they knew about schools was the experiences they had as students. We engaged in this topic at length because board members could understand and thus have informed opinions on it. Over time, I began to notice this was a pattern. When I had what I would refer to as a "good" and "supportive" board, they offered strong opinions only on topics they could understand.

CHALLENGES OF SCHOOL BOARDS

There are five common qualifications most states have to become a school board member. A school board member must be a registered voter and live in the district in which they are running. In addition, they must have a high school diploma or certificate of high school equivalency. Lastly, they must not have been convicted of a felony and must not be a current employee of the school district.

This is a pretty minimal set of qualifications for those we trust with some very important responsibilities. It is the equivalent of corporations and non-profits leaving themselves open to the possibility that their board of directors may be filled with low-skilled or irrelevantly skilled CEOs.

Perhaps this wouldn't be an issue if voters took their responsibilities at the ballot box seriously. If the citizens make wise decisions at the ballot box, all goes well; if not, the results can be catastrophic. Unfortunately, most citizens will not put in the time prior to the election to develop thorough knowledge of actual values, needs, and issues of the school system.

The average voter also does not take the time to come to an understanding of the personal character and capabilities of individual candidates (Spencer 2013). A significant percentage of voters will vote out of ignorance or emotion. Many will vote as they are told by friends, acquaintances, or groups to which they belong. Thus, school board composition is frequently not optimal for representing the values, needs, and wants of the larger community.

Per state statute, boards of education are commonly responsible for hiring, evaluating, and terminating the superintendent. In addition, boards are responsible for setting direction for their school district and developing policies designed to guide staff, student, parent, and community member behavior. Boards are responsible for approving the local school budget as well as having the final say over staff employment decisions. Lastly, boards approve many aspects of school operations, such as the school calendar, contracts with outside vendors, and the curriculum taught to students.

Examination of these responsibilities and the required qualifications of board members reveals a gap between the knowledge and skills required and the responsibilities assigned. Although often people of impeccable character with a deep desire to provide service, board members are simply ill-equipped to assume these responsibilities. For example, how can a school board effectively make what is arguably their most important decision, whom should they hire?

Typically, board members are expected to make this important decision without having experience as a superintendent or a clear understanding of the day-to-day requirements of the job. Some boards will use the services of a consultant. However, many times, this consultant works for a state school boards association. Often, these consultants are experienced board members, but they still do not have the knowledge or experience to understand what makes for a highly effective superintendent.

Thus, frequently, the situation is a group of underprepared volunteers making the most important decision they can make for their school community. Perhaps this could partially explain the reason for the high rate of turnover in the position of superintendent.

Another challenge is the superintendent evaluation. A well-conceived, comprehensive, and fair evaluation process based on performance must be grounded in the specific job responsibilities of the superintendent. It should be designed to encourage improvement in the superintendent's performance and, consequently, the school district's performance.

The evaluation of a superintendent's performance is a complex undertaking. Yet this process is done by community members who are untrained in evaluating professional educators and who may see the superintendent only once or twice a month. As a result, superintendents are often assessed by individuals who do not have all of the information, knowledge, or skills they need.

Board members will often substitute opinions for anecdotal evidence, be overly influenced by a few vocal chronic complaints, and make judgments unrelated to measures of success or achievement of organizational goals (Moffett 2011). Every superintendent wants a positive evaluation. A positive evaluation can be important for future job prospects. However, this evaluation is rarely comprehensive, nor does it result in the professional growth of the superintendent.

Then, there is the development of the annual school district budget. Every veteran superintendent knows that the budget will be cut by members of the board, regardless of how well that budget has been constructed. Board members need to both feel and appear like they are being careful with taxpayer money. All boards must appear conservative, so the superintendent must prepare a budget containing excess for the board to cut. You must be prepared to lose a little blood in the budget process to keep the fans happy (Black and English 2001).

Yet board members will often get bogged down in costs they do not understand. The approval of an entire budget can be held up because a few board members don't think the front office needs a postage machine. Not only is this cost insignificant in the big picture of the larger budget; secretarial staff are very busy and cannot afford to spend their time going back and forth on a regular basis to the post office. Things that appear to be no big deal or unnecessary to an outsider can be very important to those who work in a school system.

Superintendents are not in the business of making or saving money. We are in the business of educating children. Our top priority must be to ensure that each and every child has the best future we can secure from the taxpayer. However, of course we must be responsible with the funds we secure and use them wisely.

The board can and should hold the administration responsible for appropriate use of district funds, but they do not have the knowledge required to evaluate the items that should compose that budget. Annually, veteran superintendents play the game of creating an initial budget with surplus and then hope they can lead board members to make cuts in the areas they know are the fluff.

IMPACT ON SUPERINTENDENTS

As these three examples show, almost every aspect of school board members' responsibility requires knowledge and skills that board members simply do not have. If they contain their role to representing the community interests and values, ask good and frequent questions, provide oversight, and trust the experts, they can have a positive impact on school systems. Of course, it is even better when there is a supportive board president, a strong board nucleus, and stable board composition. However, when boards attempt to go beyond these roles, they can thwart progress and create chaos.

Superintendents cite governance as the most significant obstacle to school improvement. A national survey conducted by Public Agenda found that nearly 70 percent of superintendents say their boards interfere when they shouldn't and two-thirds believe "too many school boards would rather hire a superintendent they can control." Even in the best of times, there are tensions due to blurred lines regarding roles and responsibilities (Melton et al. 2019).

An otherwise ethical board member may attempt to cross the line on occasion. They will push the boundaries in an effort to get something of value for themselves. For example, they may try to block the hiring of a new teacher because another candidate that was not offered the job would have been an excellent high school coach for a sport their child excels in. Even though the district has a problem with unexcused absences, they may advocate strongly against strengthening board policy in this area because annually they take an extended vacation with their family while school is in session. Perhaps they request a late change in the date of graduation so that in-laws from out of town can attend the event. Maybe they request preferential treatment to influence the selection of the teacher their child will have for a subject area.

While uncomfortable, these situations are usually isolated events, and, in general if the board member does not get what they want, they do not get too upset. Unlike the exploitive, evil board member we will discuss in the next chapter, retribution against those who stand in the way of these single-issue offenders is generally light.

SOLUTIONS

Nothing can make life better for a harried superintendent than a board that is united behind them. Nothing can make life more miserable than a badly divided board that routinely questions every action and decision. Effectively managing a board is essential for success as a superintendent. There are several guidelines a superintendent can follow to strengthen and preserve relationships with well-intentioned, reasonably sane board members.

Board members will spontaneously raise ludicrous ideas at board meetings without thinking through the consequences of their statements. Instead of putting them on the spot by pointing out the flaws in their ideas, acknowledge their statement and tell them you will look into it. A few days later, follow up with them, and it is very likely they no longer will want you to pursue the idea. If they do want to pursue the idea further, then it is time to do your due diligence and place it on the agenda for discussion with the full board.

I cannot reiterate enough how many times a spontaneous idea put forth at a board meeting was quickly forgotten about. If I had argued every idea raised, I would have fostered hard feelings, and, if I had followed up on every idea immediately, I would have wasted a tremendous amount of valuable time. Sometimes, acknowledging and then delaying is your best strategy.

When it comes to questionable board member behavior, allow other board members to confront the issue. If a board member is making an unreasonable request of you, remind them that you work for the board as a whole and that their request should be made through the board president. If the request is unreasonable and the board is functional, board members will deal with their colleagues. It is more difficult to see the superintendent as the sole source of the problem when the board itself is confronting the member.

When making difficult decisions, put board members in conflict with the facts, not with you personally. If you need to make a recommendation that will be controversial, provide facts that support and mirror that recommendation. Keep the focus of the discussion on those facts, and this will keep the issue from becoming about you.

A strategic plan can be a valuable tool for keeping parties on the same page. When you work with stakeholders to develop a strategic plan and have it approved by the board, it can help to keep board member actions focused. When a board member wants to go in an errant direction, the superintendent and other board members can use the plan to redirect them to their already established commitments.

Superintendents or their subordinates are often guilty of seeking to share their wealth of knowledge about an issue. Sometimes, they forget that board members, who usually have a life and responsibilities outside of their board membership, want only a little background and the bottom line. This is especially true when it comes to presentations made at board meetings.

When a simple question is answered with more than any person wanted to know, superintendents or subordinates can come across as know-it-all blowhards. If you or someone on your staff makes lengthy presentations filled with abundant, tangentially related facts and information, the board will resent you for wasting their time. When you have the choice between saying more or less, always say less. If they want to know more information, they can ask.

With the exception of communication with the board president over specific items and returning phone calls initiated by individual board members, always communicate with each board member equally. If you provide information to one member, then you should provide it to all. You never want to create the perception that you are treating board members differently. Perceived differential treatment will likely lead to suspicion and resentment.

Board members sometimes contact a principal or a staff member directly. This makes sense when the issue is specific to their own child. Board members' children should never be treated any better or worse than other children in the school district. Board members must be able to appropriately exercise their responsibilities as parents. However, they should not have direct contact with staff members about other school-related issues. Taking this action puts staff members in a very uncomfortable position and undermines the authority of the superintendent.

Make sure your board policies clearly articulate a chain of command so that board members feel confident about what to say when a community member contacts them with a problem. Also make sure that your administrative staff knows to direct board members' concerns about issues that are not directly related to board members' children to your office.

Always stay out of board elections. The last thing you want to do is to publicly back one candidate or group of candidates over another and then have them lose. Not only is this unethical and inappropriate; the new slate will certainly make you pay for backing the wrong horse. This does not mean that you can't encourage community members you think would be good board members to seek election. Sometimes, planting the seed through some encouraging words will yield a positive and productive board of education member.

A word of caution regarding some groups that tend to become bad board members. First, because most teachers have an anti-administration bias and view the system from the isolation of the classroom, they tend to make bad board members. Second, those in positions that require or promote giving one-way directives with the expectation that those directives will be followed, tend to be bad board members. Law enforcement officers, physicians, and military officers tend to have difficulty with the give-and-take involved in board meetings.

On the other hand, fellow school administrators at any level and those who work in team-based environments tend to make pretty decent board members. They are used to the give-and-take of argumentation and compromise.

Lastly, you need to know the hills you are willing to die on. For me, I will hold the line when the issue is a potential ethical violation or when the best interests of students are clearly not being considered. I am all in on my advocacy and, if necessary, opposition for these types of issues. On the other hand, if the issue does not focus on the needs of students and is not unethical, I will demonstrate great flexibility and deference to the board's wishes.

You can lose by winning too much too often (Black and English 2001). Even when you get the outcome you seek, you must try not to appear to defeat those who are on the other side of the issue. What a board member believes about an issue is their truth, no matter how misinformed they may be. This is especially true with new board members who may have heard stories about your leadership style. Listen actively, and try to use what you learn to persuade them. If you cannot change their perception, agree to disagree without being disagreeable. In the end, by the authority granted to them, the board is always right, even when they are wrong.

CONCLUSION

Most board members are hard-working individuals who have made the decision to serve their communities. They do so at great sacrifice of time and sometimes standing among other members of the community. They seek to do what they believe is best for children; they simply do not have the knowledge or skills to handle the complex responsibilities they are given in today's highly complex educational environment. The better educated and trained your school board members are in the work of governance, the more likely they are to assist you in helping the district perform at a high level.

Occasionally an otherwise "good" board member will forget that they serve the interests of all children and will go rogue to represent their own interests or the interests of groups they are a part of. Instead of protecting the school district from political pressures, they have become a conduit for such pressure. When the overall board dynamics are healthy, these situations can be handled with minimal damage to the superintendent.

The overall dynamics of the board and support for the superintendent can be improved and maintained by a superintendent who handles the board with skill. An undermanaged board can easily get out of control, doing considerable damage to the overall school system. However, there is little that can be done when evil, exploitive individuals assume control of the board. In this case, a school district can go from the penthouse to the outhouse in a relatively short period of time.

KEY POINTS OF THIS CHAPTER

- The composition of the school board is frequently not optimal for representing the values, needs, and wants of the larger community.

- Although often people of impeccable character with a deep desire to provide service, board members are simply ill-equipped to assume the responsibilities assigned to them by legal statute.
- If a board contains their role to representing the community interests and values, asking good and frequent questions, providing oversight, and trusting the experts, they can have a positive impact on school systems. If they go beyond this role, they can create chaos and thwart progress.
- A critical skill for a superintendent is to learn to manage their boss.
- In the end, by the authority granted to them, the board is always right, even when they are wrong.

QUESTIONS FOR DISCUSSION OR REFLECTION

1. How will you handle the fact that board members are given statutory responsibilities that they typically do not have the knowledge or skill to complete?
2. How will you respond when an otherwise "good" board member makes a request that is inappropriate or unethical?
3. What are your "hills to die on"? When will you oppose board members' potential actions?
4. In addition to the strategies presented, what other strategies will you use to manage the effectiveness of your school board?

Truth Six

You Cannot Defeat an Evil, Exploitive Board Majority

> Many times, the first person on the exploitive board member's hitlist is the Superintendent.
>
> —Spencer

Imagine the following scenario. An individual seeks election to the school board to fulfill a personal need. In this case the need is for power, control, self-esteem, and social stature. Through a campaign of false and distorted information, she is able to gain a seat on the board. Although her official actions are kept in check by the majority of the board, she uses her first year to publicly and privately undermine the board. She learns the board's vulnerabilities and uses this information to make fellow board members and the district administration look bad.

When the next election cycle comes around, she has recruited others to run that share her agenda. They violate campaign election laws and board policies as well as use tactics that include deception, lying, and fooling people into thinking they can solve all of the school district's problems. They know the buzz words to use like "we will lower everyone's taxes" and "raise everyone's standardized test scores to make them equal to the best school districts in the state." It does not matter that these are false promises; they are the types of statements that the community likes to hear.

Their opposition, constrained by self-imposed boundaries of honesty and decency, continues to display honorable and respectable behavior. Their honest statements and unwillingness to sling mud are at least partially responsible for their defeat at the ballot box. A new majority of the board is established. Despite having four members remaining that have served at least two terms, they use their power to elect a president with one year of experience and a vice president with no board experience.

The first person the new majority targets for elimination is the district superintendent. They use spies within the staff to gain information. They harass the superintendent and her staff by making extraordinary requests for information that they subsequently do not use. Every chance they get, they make it their mission to question the superintendent's decisions and make her look bad publicly. Attempts to use policies to constrain their behavior are met with changes to the very bylaws that govern their behavior. Eventually, other holdover board members resign out of frustration, further cementing their hold of power.

At the same time, they continue to promote all of the great things they are doing to the public. They set up special Facebook groups to share all of their achievements. They are prominent at every school event, never being shy to share the great work they are doing on behalf of the children in the district. The public takes their statements at face value, never questioning their true motives.

The superintendent eventually quits and finds a job elsewhere. A new superintendent is hired that will do their bidding. This superintendent is willing to undermine the current district administrative staff at the same time they give extra authority to the loyal staff spies. These spies are enabled to do things that are best for them and their friends but are not in the best interest of students or all of the staff.

As a result of this new system of rewarding loyal spies, longtime district administrators seek employment elsewhere. High-level talent is lost, the culture becomes counterproductive to focusing on student needs, and eventually the district's reputation suffers. It becomes difficult to attract new talent as the district withers from within. By the time the community realizes the damage done, it is too late. They have been fooled by con artists who never intended to serve the needs of the greater good. These individuals were in it only to meet their own needs and the needs of groups they are members of.

Something like this should never happen in a school district. Schools should be a place where we put aside political differences to provide children with the best future possible. Unfortunately, this type of scenario happens more frequently than the general public suspects. How and why does it happen?

CHALLENGES OF EVIL, EXPLOITIVE BOARD MAJORITIES

Individuals run for school board election for a variety of reasons. They may have children in the district and want to have a direct impact on the quality of education they receive. They may have political ambitions for which the school board is a stepping-stone. A community member may simply want to provide service and believe that they can make a positive difference in the quality of education the district is providing.

It is also possible that they run for the school board to seek revenge against a teacher, administrator, or coach. Yet even another possibility is that they see board membership as on opportunity to offer employment to friends or relatives. Lastly, a board candidate may seek election because they have a need to feel important or powerful or to be in control. The nature and quality of the service they provide will depend on the personal importance and nature of their reasons for seeking election.

Those that grossly abuse and misuse an honorable position of service to fill some void or unmet need that exists in their lives are evil, exploitive board members. However, even within this category there is a spectrum. Some evil and exploitive board members will expend a reasonable degree of effort to provide a quality education for children while quietly seeking to meet their own need. Others, who seem to be fueled by an insatiable desire for power and control, will spend much of their energies to establish complete dominance of everyone and everything in the school district (Spencer 2013).

To get on the inside of board actions, the evil exploiter must win the election. To do this requires developing a thorough understanding of and subsequently taking action on the public's frailties and vulnerabilities. The evil exploiter knows that they can cultivate votes by capitalizing on the fear, insecurity, unmet needs, and other human emotions that compel otherwise uninformed voters. If necessary, anxieties will be created where none exist.

Evil, exploitive board candidates will capitalize on the fears and insecurities of the public by bringing attention to embellished or imagined issues (Spencer 2013). They will cast themselves as the saviors who can make all of the problems and worries go away. They get elected on campaigns consisting of fear and lies.

Once the primary defense mechanism for the school district, the election process, has been successfully breached, the newly elected evil exploiter is no longer on the outside. With limited opportunities to accomplish anything on their own, they must now work from the inside to expand their influence. Often quietly at first, they will ask questions and seek information. Unlike board members who seek to facilitate improvements, they will gather information to identify weaknesses and vulnerabilities. They will size up the fortitude of potential foes and continue cultivating allies.

Evil, exploitive board members need to establish a support and protection system. This may start with the attempted use of manipulation skills with current board members. If they are unsuccessful conning and schmoozing board colleagues, they will take a more aggressive approach. They will use whatever means necessary to undermine the public's perception of the credibility and the effectiveness of the current board members.

At the same time, they will cultivate allies within the school system. They will seek and then use information they can exploit. Disgruntled staff members will provide this information and share their grievances because they believe that the evil, exploitive board member will protect or promote their interests. These types of board members will present the negative information they gather in a distorted and often incomplete manner. In addition, they will emphasize this information repeatedly and publicly.

Evil, exploitive board members will also continue cultivating community support. Building on the façade established during their campaign, they will use every opportunity to demonstrate that they and not the other members of the board are the unwavering champions of the public. They will cast themselves as victims of the current board composition: if only the board would listen to me, we would be able to do what is best for kids. If they are unable to establish enough influence on the current board, they will seek like-minded community members to run for a seat on the board. The election tactics used successfully the first time will be enhanced and then repeated.

Regardless of how it happens, if an evil, exploitive board member is able to seize control over the majority of the board, their next step will be the elimination of adversaries. Those who see these individuals for what they are will seek to stop them. By speaking up or resisting actions, they have become the enemy.

Unlike those constrained by self-imposed boundaries of fair play; professionalism; and respectable, honorable behavior, the evil and exploitive board member will do whatever is necessary to destroy their opponents. They have an uncontestable advantage in that there is no end to the ruthless offensiveness or cruelty they are willing to display (Spencer 2013). For their opponents, there are limits.

An offensive barrage is undertaken designed to destroy the credibility of anyone who musters the courage to seek to expose their unscrupulous behavior. When challenged for these actions, they will play the victim, hiding behind their public proclamations of doing what is in students' best interests. They will go to great lengths to discredit their accuser, foster sympathy for themselves, and eventually get their accusers to back down. Most of the time, these actions will destroy the will of the challenger to do what is good, right, and just.

You will be amazed and shocked at how evil, exploitive board members are defended by parents and patrons. Using deception and manipulation, these types of board members continue duping the naïve public into thinking they are a servant of the people, when in reality they are a servant of the self.

Sometimes, this defense is simply due to an unwillingness to admit making the wrong choice in the election. People take pride in the belief that they made the right choice when they cast their ballot (Spencer 2013). This is despite the fact that they spent very little if any time and effort researching the candidates. Out of a sense of vanity, some individuals continue to publicly support an evil, exploitive board member because they simply cannot admit they were wrong.

Others who witness the attacks launched by evil, exploitive board members and the results of those attacks do not want to become targets. They have seen the lengths evil and exploitive board members will go to destroy reputations and careers. They will choose self-preservation or self-interests and will abandon any thoughts of confrontation, thus further eliminating any constraints on the behavior of an evil, exploitive board majority.

IMPACT ON SUPERINTENDENTS

If the opponent of an evil, exploitive board majority is a superintendent with character and conviction who chooses not to comply with the unethical, unprofessional, or illegal demands placed upon them, they are destined to be neutralized or forced out. By choosing to remain true to themselves, their value systems, and the ethics of the profession, they become a top target for elimination. With the board's authority to hire and fire the superintendent, the torture and eventual separation of the educational leader begins.

Eventually, those who are perceived as loyal to the departed superintendent become the new targets. Witnesses to the carnage, other school leaders will be undermined and will either choose to leave or will be replaced. Their positions will be filled with loyalists who do not have courage, conviction, and the desire to adhere to professional standards. Often, the result of these personnel changes is the establishment of situational application of the procedures and standards that define the policies of the school system.

If a board policy does not fit the needs of the evil, exploitive majority, they will change that policy to suit their needs. If they cannot change the policy, then they will selectively enforce it. No longer will the administration hold all students and all staff universally accountable. Instead, standards will now apply to some situations and some people. Spies and loyalists under the protective wing of an evil, exploitive board majority will become untouchable.

Eventually, there becomes a noticeable group of insiders and outsiders. It may take time, but the school system will erode into one fertile for backstabbing, throat cutting, and opportunism. Disgusted by unethical and unprofessional behavior, the pride and loyalty of those on the outside diminish. Their commitment to students and the community reduces, resulting in a negative impact on effectiveness and productivity. Those who can will flee to pursue new opportunities. The overall quality of educational leaders and staff diminishes, which eventually results in a decline in the experience of students. When the community finally realizes what has happened, it is usually too late.

A superintendent in this type of situation has three choices. First, they can be true to themselves, their convictions, and their personal and professional value system. They can say no to unethical, inappropriate, or illegal demands. Courageous leaders who choose this option will prod the wrath of the evil, exploitive board members.

Second, they can kowtow by renouncing their personal and professional value system. They can do what they are told. They can comply with requests out of a sheer desire to retain their position.

Third, they can set aside personal and professional standards for the time being and hope that things will get better. They hope that they can wait out the evil, exploitive board majority with the hope that eventually things will get better.

Unfortunately, none of these choices are destined for positive outcomes. If the superintendent chooses to honor themselves and stay true to their personal and professional value system, it is very likely their career and physical and emotional health will suffer. There will never be enough hours in the day to combat the toxicity of evil, exploitive board members. They will prepare, work, plot, pillage, or plunder harder and longer than you can possibly imagine. Eliminating you becomes their full-time job, and they will work overtime to destroy you (Coda and Jetter 2016).

If they choose to dishonor themselves by disavowing their professional and personal values, most times, their career will be severely tarnished and will die anyway. If they choose to bow down temporarily, then one by one the respect of professional colleagues and members of the staff will be lost.

SOLUTIONS

Unfortunately, there are no actions a superintendent can take when an evil, exploitive board majority assumes control. They are the employer, and thus ultimately they have the authority. All a superintendent can hope to do is to minimize the personal and professional damage. However, there are legislative actions that could be taken to improve this situation. This type of situation cannot be resolved without better statutory controls over board actions.

Every school board should have an outside entity with appropriate authority that monitors certain aspects of their work. Perhaps this outside group could consist of an equal number of retired school administrators and retired board members selected because of their record of distinguished service. This outside board could report directly to a county or state education official who is given the authority to intervene when necessary.

No board of education should be allowed to change their own bylaws without the approval of this outside entity. Allowing boards to change their bylaws through a simple majority vote enables them to eliminate checks on their own behavior. Currently, a simple majority of the board can change their bylaws to meet their own needs without any outside constraints ensuring the changes are appropriate.

Furthermore, this outside entity should conduct or at a minimum review the board evaluation. Allowing boards to complete their own evaluation is ludicrous. Not only is this sometimes never completed, frequently it represents only the majority view of the board. If the majority view consists of evil and exploitive board members, how can the results be valid or useful for district improvement? Evaluation data from every board member, including members of the board minority, should be shared publicly.

In addition, superintendents should be able to submit concerns related to board behavior to this outside group. This outside board could then investigate and draw independent conclusions and recommendations. Perhaps this will eliminate all of the costly buyouts boards reach with current superintendents. All of these actions would provide checks and balances beyond the ballot box.

Until changes in legislation like those proposed are enacted, the only good choice left for the superintendent is to update their resume and seek employment elsewhere. This is the subject of our next chapter.

CONCLUSION

The vast majority of individuals who seek to serve as board members do so for noble reasons. Unfortunately, there are also those who seek board service as a means to fill personal needs or desires. While the path may vary in substance, the overall process for how an evil, exploitive board majority eventually ruins a school district is predictable.

First, in an attempt to cultivate votes by capitalizing on fear or concerns, an election campaign based on lies and partial truths is undertaken. Because of the lack of time most citizens put in researching candidates, those who claim to be the solution to all of the district's problems win election. Once on the inside, the newly elected members gain access to information they use against the school system. At the same time, they continue expanding their influence by building alliances with those who are disgruntled or ambitious.

If they are unable to gain the influence necessary for control, they will do whatever is necessary to appear like victims of the current board. They will take advantage of every opportunity to publicly appear like the only board members who care about staff, students, and the community. If necessary, they will recruit and support like-minded candidates for board election.

Once an evil, exploitive board majority takes hold, the quest for eliminating adversaries begins. Usually, the superintendent and those who are seen as loyal to the superintendent are the first targets for elimination. The superintendent and their top leadership team members are eventually replaced with those who are loyal to the evil, exploitive board majority. These loyalists facilitate a school culture and climate that leads to a decline in the quality of education provided to students.

As predictable as the general path of destruction is, so is the impact it has on a superintendent. If a superintendent is unfortunate enough to be the leader of a school district in a community that allows an evil, exploitive board majority to assume control, there is no good solution. The best a superintendent in this situation can do is to recognize the situation early and take action to seek employment elsewhere. The only hope for improving this situation lies with strengthening external controls over local school board behavior.

KEY POINTS OF THIS CHAPTER

- Those who abuse and misuse an honorable position of service to fill some void or unmet need that exists in their lives are evil, exploitive board members.
- The evil exploiter knows that they can cultivate votes by capitalizing on the fear, insecurity, unmet needs, and other human emotions that compel otherwise uninformed voters.
- Once elected, if their agenda is thwarted, they will cast themselves as victims of the current board composition.
- Unlike those constrained by self-imposed boundaries of fair play; professionalism; and respectable, honorable behavior, evil and exploitive board members will do whatever is necessary to destroy their opponents.
- If that opponent is a superintendent with character and conviction who chooses not to comply with the unethical, unprofessional, or illegal demands placed upon them, they are destined to be neutralized or forced out.
- Often, the result of the purge of top district leaders is the establishment of situational application of the procedures and standards that define the policies of the school system.
- It may take time, but the school system will erode into one fertile for backstabbing, throat cutting, and opportunism.
- Every school board should have an outside entity with appropriate authority that monitors certain aspects of their work.

QUESTIONS FOR DISCUSSION OR REFLECTION

1. If you are confronted with an evil, exploitive board majority, what would you do?
2. Do you agree that an outside entity consisting of retired, distinguished board members and superintendents could serve as a check on bad board behavior? If so, why don't you think such an entity already exists?
3. What, if any, other strategies can you come up with to either effectively cope with or prevent evil, exploitive board majorities?

Truth Seven

There Is a Strong Chance Your Tenure Will Not Last Forever

> Every relationship is temporary and every career comes to an end.
> —Evert and Van Deuren

It is late at night, and you are watching national election results on the television. Your phone rings, and it is your board secretary on the line. Her tone of voice gives you an indication the news is not good. In a surprise, all three of the incumbent board members have lost their seats to candidates who ran on a platform highly critical of both the superintendent and the school district. That means that the board majority will now consist of five out of nine members who do not respect or value the work you have done in the district. As you attempt to go to sleep, you realize the first task on tomorrow's to-do list is updating your resume.

CHALLENGES OF JOB SECURITY

Every superintendent's tenure will come to an end. This end may be a bittersweet if not joyous occasion. Perhaps it is a retirement undertaken on your own terms or the acceptance of a new, desirable position elsewhere. Other times, the ending may be acrimonious with no love lost between the board and the superintendent. If your experience is like that of the average superintendent, your tenure will last between three and seven years. Thus, if you have a fifteen-year career as a superintendent, it is likely to be served in two to five school districts. Superintendents are the modern-day nomads of education.

On the one hand, the departure may be abrupt. This is obviously the case when malfeasance is uncovered. Often, this is also the case when an issue or crisis in the district spins out of control and the board or community looks for someone to blame. The superintendent becomes the scapegoat.

On the other hand, various scenarios can result in a departure that occurs over a more extended period of time. With each successive board election, the superintendent may have a board that is a little less supportive. Over the course of several election cycles, the superintendent simply may no longer be a good match for the board or community priorities.

Perhaps the superintendent used all of their political capital and goodwill to accomplish an important change in the district. As a result of leading the charge to pass a divisive referendum or school redistricting plan, the superintendent may have called in all of their favors and have nothing left to lean on when the next issue arises.

Maybe, out of the courage of their convictions, the superintendent took a stand on a controversial staff or community issue. By telling people what they needed to hear instead of what they wanted to hear, the superintendent rubbed too many people the wrong way.

Possibly the superintendent took a risk or made a mistake that resulted in a negative outcome. This negative outcome stoked a strong negative emotional reaction from district stakeholders. Soon, past problems are resurrected to bolster arguments for change at the top. Sadly, for some, destroying our professional career is a game (Polka and Litchka 2008). They are the top dog, so let's get them!

Regardless of the reason or timing, every superintendent moves on professionally at some point. It is the rare individual who is immune. Knowing this inevitability, it is unfortunate that, as part of preparation programs, superintendents are not prepared for how to effectively handle this situation.

IMPACT ON SUPERINTENDENTS

There are three overlapping stages that characterize the majority of departures. First is the recognition phase. This is the phase in which a decision is made, by you or for you, that it is time to leave. Second is the disengagement phase. This is the phase in which you begin to formulate a plan for your exit. The final phase is recovery and reflection. In this phase, you recharge your emotional reserves and learn from your experience. Hopefully, you emerge wiser and ready to take on the next challenge.

Recognizing each stage and taking the necessary actions can improve the quality of the transition for both you and the school district. Early recognition of an impending need for departure is critical. While there are a few sure signs that a departure is imminent, it is usually an accrual of events and actions that signal it is time to leave. For example:

- Board members accept as a fact rumors about you or your motives for recommending a course of action.
- Your recommendations on a number of minor issues are debated at length and result in split votes.
- The board wants to meet without you present for an extended executive session.
- Retired board members or staff begin to regularly show up at board meetings to question your recommendations.
- The board regularly wants more and more information before it decides on matters.
- The board has spies in your administration who share information with them behind your back.
- The board fails to discipline one of its own members who continuously violates board ethics.
- Information is being shared in the public that was known only to members of the administration and the school board.
- You are on the receiving end of a number of edgy questions.
- Staff members or the school attorney start to act differently toward you, perhaps not taking your directives or inquiries seriously.
- Without good reason, a board member files an ethics complaint against you or requests that an outside entity scrutinize some aspect of school district operations.
- The board requests a morale survey be done with staff and then uses the information gained to chastise your leadership style in public.
- Normally short board meetings begin to last for inordinate amounts of time.

Any combination of these events should set off the alarm bells for a superintendent that an impending storm is gathering. Oftentimes, superintendents wait too long, hoping that things will get better. Instead, they need to listen to that tiny voice we all have inside our head that something isn't quite right.

This is the time to recognize the warning signs of any unfixable aspects of the situation and move forward in a way that causes minimal damage to the school district as well as the career the individual has worked so hard to develop. In short, this is the time to update your resume and develop your exit strategy.

However, this is not the time to waver. Instead, this is the time to stand tall, maintain excellence, set the organization up for future success, and give the organization everything it requires of you. Just because you find yourself in turmoil doesn't give you the freedom to show weakness or reduce yourself to similar petty or hurtful behaviors.

It is also not the time to whine or complain about how unfair the situation has become. You aren't going to change any minds, and you will lose your dignity. In fact, most community members and employees will not even care that you are leaving. There is no such thing as institutional loyalty (Black and English 2001). If you want loyalty, you need to get a dog. Generally speaking, you came into the position alone, and subsequently you will leave the position alone.

SOLUTIONS

A person is remembered for how they enter and how they exit. Exit with grace, remaining a professional until the end. This will help protect your reputation, and you may need the best recommendation possible from some of those board members to find your next position. Burn bridges at your own peril. With the exception of emotional satisfaction, there is little to be gained from scorching the earth.

It is important to remember that at times like these, no matter how good your relationship has been, the board attorney works for the board. It is their responsibility to represent the board's interests, not yours. They want to maintain their status of providing services to their client, so do not expect them to be on your side. If your situation requires legal representation, then you must obtain your own legal counsel.

Related to this is the pursuit of litigation. In the remote case you have legal action you seek to take, you do not want to tip your hand and give the board time to prepare their case against you. Threatening legal action is ill advised. It is better to speak to a lawyer or your professional association.

Unless you have a strong legal position that can prove wrongful termination, or you have no intentions of seeking future employment in education, it is usually not a good idea to pursue legal action. Potential employers will not look favorably upon your suing your last board.

As you begin the search for a new position, keep it as low profile as possible. Of course, this is difficult to do in the age of the internet. Assume that everyone talks to everyone, and keep your mouth shut. If your current board learns that you are looking for employment elsewhere, it will likely accelerate your exit.

Whether you reach a negotiated settlement to separate from service or you leave for a new position, your tenure in that district has come to an end. It is now time to recover from and reflect upon the experience. Leaving a district, even under the best of circumstances, can be an emotional experience. It is even harder when you leave due to causes that are less than ideal.

Reminding yourself that superintendent tenures are notoriously unstable and not necessarily a reflection of your worth or underlying ability is helpful for managing the turmoil inherent in the process (Evert and Van Deuren 2013). It is at this time that you must refuse to allow what has transpired to define you. While difficult, it is essential to keep a sense of perspective about all aspects of yourself, refusing to globalize or catastrophize this single event. You are not defined by what you do.

It is important to try to understand what has happened and why. You may never fully comprehend why your tenure ended. The most confident of superintendents will encounter feelings of self-doubt and inadequacy as a result of what has been experienced.

This does not mean that you cannot learn from and as a result grow from the experience. If you made a significant mistake that directly caused your tenure to come to an end, admit the mistake, and figure out what to do differently the next time. Don't beat yourself up too much. You may be wounded, but you do not have to be defeated.

Once you leave, don't look back. Adversaries developed will become even bolder in their retaliation and confrontation once you are no longer employed in the district. They will not want to see you prevail, and they will want to tarnish the exited superintendent's accomplishments at least one last time.

Shame on the superintendent who as the new leader discredits the exited superintendent. They do not know what that leader started with, faced, or accomplished and how it was done. In their need to appear as a savior, they buy in to the façade and disrespect the hard work of their predecessor. Do not be that person.

CONCLUSION

The length of tenure of the superintendent position is notoriously unstable and unpredictable. From the first day you assume the role, recognize that you are replaceable and eventually you will depart from the district. During time in the role, the superintendent must do everything they can to improve the quality of education provided to students. Yet, at some point, the superintendent must also recognize when it is time to move on.

Upon recognizing the need to move on, it is important to plan your exit strategy. The ultimate goal of this strategy is a graceful exit that does minimal harm to the district and keeps as many relationships intact as possible. After exiting, it is helpful to engage in reflection so that you can learn from the experience. In addition, if it is at all possible, the superintendent should find a way to take a short period of time off. These transitions are highly emotional experiences that require time to decompress before jumping into something new. Hopefully recharged and wiser, the superintendent can now move on to their next position, continuing to make a difference in the lives of students.

KEY POINTS OF THIS CHAPTER

- Superintendents are the modern-day nomads of education.
- There are typically three phases to a superintendent's departure: recognition, disengagement, and recovery/reflection.
- Recognize the warning signs of the unfixable aspects of a situation, and move forward in a way that causes minimal damage to the school district and your career.
- Burn bridges at your own peril. With the exception of emotional satisfaction, there is little to be gained from scorching the earth.
- The board attorney is not your attorney and does not represent your interests.
- The most confident of superintendents will encounter feelings of self-doubt and inadequacy as a result of what has been experienced.
- Once you leave, don't look back.

QUESTIONS FOR DISCUSSION OR REFLECTION

1. How will you prepare for the fact that it is inevitable that your tenure will come to an end?
2. When the time comes, how will you ensure that you exit with grace and dignity?

Truth Eight

It Is Lonely at the Top

> You will never know who your friends are while you occupy a position of power.
>
> —Dotlich, Noel, and Walker

It is late in the school year, and you need to make a difficult personnel decision. One of your administrators will earn tenure if you recommend renewal of his contract. His performance has been erratic. At times, you are very confident in him to perform the job responsibilities. At other times, you question his ability to meet deadlines, follow up on assigned tasks, and hold staff and students accountable.

This decision would be easier if the individual had not been dealing with a potentially life-threatening illness for the past two years. Not only do you have empathy for his situation; you don't know how the illness has impacted upon his ability to do the job if and when his health improves. There have been periods of extended absence for very legitimate reasons.

Whom do you talk to for advice or even just to discuss this matter? It is completely inappropriate to discuss it with the administrator's colleagues. That puts them in an awkward situation and does not demonstrate your confidentiality. You don't want to discuss it with board members for fear that you will appear uncertain when you do make your recommendation. You might be fortunate enough to have the sympathetic ear of a significant other, but they will not truly understand what you are experiencing. Ultimately, you will bear this burden of leadership alone.

Truth Eight

CHALLENGES OF ISOLATION

Moving into the upper level of school district administration means moving from a single focus, such as a school building or department, to a broad focus on all aspects of the school system. Those who make the move to superintendent are usually surprised to discover that they are truly alone for the first time in their career. Up until this point, they had colleagues of equal stature and may have been part of a team. There was always someone to confide in and work with on an equal basis (Dotlich, Noel, and Walker 2004).

Unlike in their previous positions, as the top authority figure employed in the school district, the superintendent can't complain to or about other district employees in the way they may have done in the past. Because of expectations that leaders must not show vulnerability and exude confidence, typically there is no one in the district to whom they can express their concerns or doubts. In the school district, they will not have a confidante like they may have had in previous positions.

People will act differently in the superintendent's presence. Perhaps their jokes will become funnier, their insights brighter, and their views more intelligent. This will all be due to the fact that no one wants to challenge someone with their level of positional authority. Some people will be frightened or intimidated by this authority. They will avoid the superintendent or at least be very cautious in their presence. They will never know what most people who work in the district truly think of them while they occupy the position of superintendent.

IMPACT ON SUPERINTENDENTS

A superintendent is always on stage. The superintendent is always performing, always under the lights, with an audience watching every move. Everyone will judge your actions, and no conversation is ever without potential consequences.

The superintendent's job is to lead and direct. It is not to make friends and cultivate a social life with district staff. Attempting to mix the two will compromise one or the other or both.

Likewise, board of education members are not your friends. They are your boss. While you can have a positive and productive working relationship with board members, always remember that they are the evaluators of your character and performance.

Be very careful and discreet at all staff and board social events. Behavior that would be considered normal for others, such as using foul language or having an excess number of alcoholic drinks, will be noticed and scrutinized if it is done by the superintendent.

The only potential true colleagues you have are superintendents who work in other districts. Some superintendents are potentially better colleagues than others. Unfortunately, many superintendents have very large egos. As a result of their narcissism, they focus extensively on sharing their accomplishments and are not shy about letting others know how wonderful and important they are. Obviously, these individuals do not make good listeners.

Sometimes, there is professional jealousy among superintendents. Other superintendents may not want to see you succeed because they may see you as a future job competitor. Instead of celebrating your success as a colleague, they privately or sometimes even publicly undermine your accomplishments so you are less of a threat. Truly get to know a colleague before you make the mistake of trusting them as a confidante.

The times when you feel like you need the most support are likely the times you will feel the most alone. Similar to a physician who prefers to work with patients whose illness can be cured, there are educators who shun colleagues when there is chaos and the promise of success is dim (Heifetz 1994). Even some of those the superintendent may have considered friends will avoid them as if they have a contagious disease when crisis occurs. When you need the most emotional and social support is likely the time when you will feel like you are being treated as a leper in the educational community.

Far too many educational leaders do not have someone to turn to. They are without a safe, professional support system. Leadership isolation is detrimental to the superintendent's health and thus the health of the organization (Ackerman and Maslin-Ostrowski 2002).

SOLUTIONS

It is vital for superintendents to find one or more leadership confidantes with whom they can communicate about intricate leadership dilemmas and doubts. Perhaps this is a former mentor or a colleague who has demonstrated the capacity to actively listen in a discreet manner.

Even better, it is a network of colleagues through which you can find camaraderie, support, and friendship. For your mental health, you must find a safe, productive outlet through which you can express your concerns about issues.

It is also important to maintain strong personal relationships outside of the work environment. Because of the demands on their time, superintendents may neglect their social supports outside of work. In addition, experiences on the job will often carry over into nonwork experiences, including marriage, family relationships, and lifestyle choices (Polka and Litchka

2008). Be aware of this spillover effect, and do your best to separate work time from home time.

Spending quality time with loved ones is key to alleviating work-related stress and creating a positive work-life balance. Boards of education that want superintendents who are healthy and productive must encourage them to prioritize family obligations. Putting children first must include superintendents doing the same with their own children.

Professional associations should encourage these informal connections. When leaders are wounded by their work, they need to have the benefit of talking with others who understand their particular brand of pain. The need to pay attention to the emotional side of leadership, more specifically the need for sustained personal and real conversations among school leaders, is vital to the profession.

Without genuine connection and affiliation, leaders will not grow and flourish. The loneliness of the position can result in superintendents leaving the profession early and potential candidates not wanting to seek the position. To increase longevity and make the position more attractive, boards need to understand the need for and encourage superintendents to speak with colleagues on a regular basis.

CONCLUSION

This chapter has been an exploration of the potential loneliness one can experience as a superintendent. Because of the nature of the position, it is likely that a superintendent will not have colleagues in their district they can confide in. It is vital for their emotional health and thus their job performance that they develop relationships with the appropriate colleagues. In addition, a superintendent must not neglect important personal relationships. Both boards of education and professional associations can take steps to facilitate the appropriate connections and affiliations for superintendents.

There is nothing quite like sensationalized negative personal press coverage to make you feel more alone. The ability to understand and work effectively with members of the media has become a survival skill for superintendents. This is the subject of the next truth: the media do not sell truth; they sell newspapers.

KEY POINTS IN THIS CHAPTER

- A superintendent will not have a confidante like they may have had in previous positions.
- You will never know what most people who work in the district truly think of you while you occupy the position of superintendent.

- You will always be on stage.
- While you can have a positive and productive working relationship with board members, always remember that they are the evaluators of your character and performance.
- Be very careful and discreet at all staff and board social events.
- Truly get to know a colleague before you make the mistake of trusting them as a confidante.
- When you need the most emotional and social support is likely the time when you will feel like you are being treated as a leper in the educational community.
- For your mental health, you must find a safe, productive outlet through which you can express your concerns about issues.
- Boards of education that want superintendents who are healthy and productive must encourage them to prioritize family obligations.

QUESTIONS FOR DISCUSSION OR REFLECTION

1. Do you have a professional support network? If not, how can you cultivate one?
2. Do you agree that boards of education should help superintendents prioritize important personal relationships?

Truth Nine

The Media Do Not Sell the Truth; They Sell Newspapers

The truth never gets in the way of a good story.

—Black and English

You walk into your office, and your normally rock-steady secretary appears nervous. She does not make eye contact or greet you with her usually enthusiastic good morning. Your first thought is uh-oh, what now? She hands you a copy of the local paper and the headline reads: "School District Promotes Teaching of Islam."

As you scan the first paragraph, you realize the district they are talking about is yours. In a semirural, politically and religiously conservative community that is primarily white and Catholic, you know this headline isn't going to go over well. As you read the rest of the article, you learn that the source of the information is a group of disgruntled parents who are unhappy with one of your middle school social studies teacher's assignments.

You immediately check with the teacher and learn that she has been teaching about the Koran as part of a unit on the influence of religions on the development of values and decisions in classical civilizations. The teacher assures you that she is not promoting the religion in her lessons; rather, she is explaining how Islam shaped decisions and actions in prior civilizations.

She has already addressed several other religions, including Judaism and Buddhism. After she identifies the relevant state curriculum standards for you, you realize that she is both surprised by this accusation and as a nontenured teacher is terrified of what this means for her future.

Next, you either return the calls to the board members who have already called you or reach out to the ones who have not called yet. You share what you have learned and what actions you intend to take next. In your phone conversations, you learn that the community member leading the charge lost a relative in the 9/11 attack on New York City.

Soon, this story has gained national media attention. You are receiving requests for television interviews as well as requests for comment from print media. Hate mail as well as letters of support are sent to your email account from all across the nation. You juggle the requests at the same time you prepare to present the facts at a special community meeting.

After reviewing all of the state standards and all of the material the teacher used, including the assignment in question, you feel confident that you can present the case that the district is not promoting any religious beliefs. Interviews with students reveal that the teacher provided facts and did not espouse opinions about the value of one religion over another.

The night of the community meeting comes and goes. After presenting the facts, several members of the community make accusations about the district and the teacher. However, most of the community members seem satisfied with the explanation and are thankful for the information. The next day, the same local newspaper has a different headline about your district: "Superintendent of ____ Does Not Believe Religion Belongs in Schools."

As you read this headline and recap of the meeting from the previous evening, you shake your head and say here we go again. All of this attention because a teacher taught content required by state standards.

CHALLENGES OF MEDIA RELATIONS

The last thing a superintendent wants to hear from their secretary is that there is a reporter waiting on hold to speak with them. Confronted with this situation, a superintendent will experience "media phobia." Immediately they will start to think, what is this about? Why? What am I going to say? If you have been a superintendent for any length of time, you will experience this phenomenon.

Reporters have a job to do. There are some in this profession who are people of great integrity who try hard to get their stories correct and make their commentaries useful. Unfortunately, there are also those who follow the mantra "if it bleeds, it leads." They will write stories that describe a situation in your school district or about you without ever asking for you to comment. They will take potshots at you under the guise that you are a public figure and therefore are open to these types of attacks.

While reporters may not write positive stories about your school district, they will certainly inquire about negative news. Typically, no matter how unprecedented or unique, positive stories are often not given attention. Meanwhile, negative news gains an inordinate amount of attention.

IMPACT ON SUPERINTENDENTS

When these stories provide insufficient information, unsubstantiated allegations, absurd analogies, biased perspectives, secondary rather than primary sources, and selectivity rather than objectivity, it can be extremely frustrating. Often, the best we can hope for is fair, balanced coverage of our school districts. Learning how to work with the media increases the chances we will receive this type of coverage.

Working effectively with the media begins with understanding what they want. They do not seek highly complex problems characterized by a high degree of ambiguity. These types of articles take up too much print space and are too difficult to explain to the average reader. Rather, they want something that can easily be understood by the average person.

Reporters want a simple story line that can be captured in a few paragraphs. Within these paragraphs, they want some quotes that will spice up the story as well a hook to use as an eye-catching headline. This is what they want, and they will seek to get it from you.

When dealing with the press, you must be perceived as open and not fearful. Those who appear defensive become worthy targets of further investigation. Unless it is a matter you are legally prohibited from addressing, never provide a blanket statement of no comment. Even then, make it a point to emphasize the reason you can't comment on the matter.

In addition, always return phone calls to reporters in as short an amount of time as possible. They may be facing deadlines, and it is likely in your best interest to squash rumors or deal with factual inaccuracies before the story goes to print. No one reads the retractions.

Do not attempt to avoid the press; they will think you are hiding something. As Black and English (2001) so eloquently stated, "reporters can be the proctologists of the print world." Obviously, you would like to avoid this kind of examination, so don't give them any reason to believe you are keeping secrets from them.

SOLUTIONS

When you do talk to the press, there are two rules to follow. First, you never talk longer than you need to, and you never volunteer information that you don't have to. Most of the questions reporters ask are simple because they want simple answers. If the reporter is satisfied with your answer, they will move on; if they are not, they will ask a follow-up question.

Sometimes, they will purposefully pause to create an awkward silence. They hope that this discomfort will cause you to reveal additional information. A superintendent can choose to wait them out, or they can ask if they have any additional questions. Do not fall into this trap by offering unsolicited information.

Many times, the reporter is on a fishing expedition for information. They do not know exactly what they are looking for and have not thought through their line of questions. They say the first thing that pops into their head, hoping that you will offer information they can use. The superintendent must not take the bait and instead must answer the question as succinctly as possible.

Unless it is an emergency situation, a reporter should always have to make an appointment to speak with you. Instruct your secretary to let the interested reporter know that they will have to squeeze them in to your already tight schedule. Knowing that time is limited will force the reporter to get to the point and then get out of your office. If there is less time for the interview, there is less time for them to snoop around for additional information.

The second rule is to always emphasize the positive aspects in your response and talk slowly. When the reporter asks you to explain why 25 percent of your students are not meeting proficiency on standardized test scores, provide an answer like, "We are very pleased that 75 percent of our students are reaching proficiency, and we will continue working hard to increase the proficiency levels of all of our students."

By reframing the question, the superintendent can answer it in a manner that emphasizes any possible positive aspect of school district performance. If you can anticipate the reporter's questions, it is helpful to develop these talking points in advance. After all, what you are saying is the truth and therefore should result in more accurate and balanced coverage of the school district. Finally, to improve the odds that you will be quoted accurately, talk slowly and repeat your statement if necessary.

Lastly, it can be helpful to get to know the members of your local media before you or your district becomes the subject of one of their stories. Invite them to meet with you for lunch so that you can get to know one another. Like any constituency, when working with the media, it helps to build relationships and establish trust prior to the time that you need them the most.

CONCLUSION

Working with the news media is a part of the job that most superintendents have no training in. In smaller districts, the superintendent is often left to use their best judgment and communication skills to serve as the district's press representative. Unfortunately, most of what reporters focus on are the salacious details of bad behavior by a district employee or the negative perceptions of some aspect of school district performance. It is frustrating that the wonderful things happening every day in our schools are ignored.

To get more fair and balanced coverage for your district, the superintendent must remain cognizant of what the reporter seeks. Then, the superintendent must follow some general guidelines for how to provide the information in the best form possible. We do not have to like dealing with the press, but they are not going away any time soon. Learning to work effectively with the press will increase the chances that you will not be going away any time soon either.

KEY POINTS IN THIS CHAPTER

- Often, the best we can hope for is fair, balanced media coverage of our school districts.
- Reporters want a simple story line that can be captured in a few paragraphs. Within these paragraphs, they want some quotes that will spice up the story as well a hook to use as an eye-catching headline.
- Never act defensive; it will only give the impression you are hiding something that requires further investigation.
- Rule number one for talking with members of the press is never talk longer than you need to and never volunteer information you don't have to.
- Rule number two for talking with members of the press is reframe the question so that you answer in a manner that emphasizes any possible positive aspect of school district performance.

QUESTIONS FOR DISCUSSION OR REFLECTION

1. Do you have any training in how to work with the news media?

    a. Is your knowledge and skill in this area adequate?
    b. Where can you go to get this training?

2. Do you have any ideas for increasing the quantity and quality of positive press coverage for your school district?
3. How can you spread the good news if your local newspapers are not interested in sharing it?

Truth Ten

You Can Make a Difference

> For most of us, surviving is not enough. If survival were the point, in the end we would surely fail; we don't live forever.
> —Heifetz and Linsky

In the opening section of this book, I provided a job description for a superintendent of schools. I proposed that, if we were being honest, this is the job description we would use to advertise for the position. I suspect that we will never see this description in an advertisement due to the fact that it is likely no one would apply for the job.

Yet people do still apply for this position. For some, it is because of the fact that they will receive the highest level of compensation offered in the public school system. For others it will be because they will be granted the greatest amount of institutional power. Money and power used appropriately can be good things.

Yet they are not enough of a reason to cope with all of the difficulties I have described in the previous chapters of this book for any length of time. Instead, to persevere you must believe that you can and will make a significant positive difference in the future for children and subsequently the society as a whole.

The difference you make will probably not be easily measured. Trying to take satisfaction in your professional life from things like improved standardized test scores or budgets that have a minimal tax increase does not measure the good that you do. Instead, you will be remembered for how you handled yourself and how you treated others. The most important thing that others will remember about you is how you made them feel about themselves.

Those who care deeply about values and have a strong sense of purpose are a dying breed. They may be an endangered species, but they must not be allowed to become extinct. I have written this book for the dreamers and idealists who believe that it is possible to make a difference through providing students with a high-quality education. For if those who care more deeply about a district's vision, mission, and values than what is in it for themselves die off, then who will be left? In part, our future as a society depends on high-quality leadership of our school districts. This high-quality leadership can be provided, but it is challenging to say the least.

Throughout this book, I have offered suggestions and advice for typical district leadership problems. I have shared experiences and warnings in the hope that perhaps I can offer solace to veteran superintendents. My descriptions are not meant to scare off those who are considering becoming a superintendent. Instead, I seek to make sure that those who seek to become a school superintendent go into the position with their eyes wide open. I sincerely hope that board members, as well as members of the public, read this so that they can gain an appreciation for the lives and challenges of their educational leaders.

THE IMPORTANCE OF CORE VALUES

I have learned some things about what I think makes someone an effective district leader. While I have not always lived up to these ideals, I do believe they are worth striving to achieve. In reality, I have made mistakes and at times been inconsistent. I have had complicated and sometimes contradictory feelings about sharing power. I have always sought to value and protect the dignity of others, yet, when I have been fearful, I have forgotten to do it.

Yet eventually I have always reminded myself of who I am and what I seek to represent as a school district leader. Especially in times of crisis and turmoil when there are no easy answers, I come back to these core values.

I believe that, when you assume a position of leadership, you assume ownership of higher standards and expectations for your actions and behavior. All school and district leadership positions require a set of competencies that must be learned and practiced. Without mastery of these basic competencies, a potential leader will be mired in management issues. Thus, these basic competencies are a prerequisite to success in school and district leadership, but they are not enough.

To achieve true and genuine leadership requires understanding and adhering to a set of core values. While each of us may have different values based on our upbringing and life experiences, I believe certain values are the core foundation upon which leadership is built.

True leaders believe that all people deserve to be treated with dignity. It does not matter what position someone holds in the organization; everyone deserves to be valued and respected. Everyone is a human being worthy of basic courtesies and must be valued for their contributions. This includes a respect for their time and efforts. True leaders never demean or devalue someone because of the position they hold in the organization, and they do not let others do it either.

True leaders believe that they must do the things they have promised they will do. Following through on promised action is the foundation of credibility. Staff and colleagues will trust you only if they know you will do what you say you will. True leaders are dependable.

True leaders are honest. Staff and colleagues will believe you only if you tell the truth. However, telling the truth is no excuse for a lack of tact. When the message is not going to be received well, it is especially important to do it as sensitively as possible. Say what you mean—just don't say it in a way that is meant to be mean.

True leaders are accountable. They do not make excuses for their actions or the actions of those they lead. Even if it is not their fault, true leaders take ownership for the outcomes of their organizations, recognizing that ultimate accountability rests with them. When you assume the role of the leader, you accept that, fair or not, you are the bottom line. The position requires that you sometimes develop Teflon for skin.

True leaders demonstrate integrity. They do the right things in the right way for the right reasons. Sometimes, this is hard. Sometimes, we may not be certain of what the right thing is, or the right thing is potentially unpopular. It is times like these that true leaders hold their ground, believing that following their moral compass is their highest priority. True leaders model the ability to do what is right in the face of controversy. This is what separates leaders from followers and critics.

True leaders take strategic risks. They do not take risks that are careless but rather those that are potentially valuable for the growth of the organization. They think through the potential benefits and consequences of potential action and then move decisively, knowing that any change will likely create uncertainty and potentially even animosity. They do this because they put the needs of their organization above all else.

True leaders persevere. Good things happen to bad people, and conversely bad things happen to good people. If you have been attacked for doing what you believe is the right course of action, then you are fully aware of this phenomenon. Making sense of this truth and turning it into a positive requires determination and a willingness not to be defeated, at least in the long run.

During difficult times, dig deep within yourself, remember why you chose to be a superintendent, and summon the energy to persevere. Self-protection makes sense; the dangers are real. But, when you cover yourself up too much, you risk losing something else. In the struggle to save yourself, you give up many of those qualities, such as purpose and passion, that are the essence of being alive.

CONCLUSION

Great managers are not always great leaders. To become a great leader requires commitment to a set of core values. These principles must guide your actions at all times, but especially difficult times. Crisis and times of great turmoil are the times when leadership is needed most. The herd instinct is strong, and a stampede not only tramples those who do not keep pace; it also makes it hard to see another direction when the dust settles. Core values will always help you find your way.

Adhere to these principles or others that represent your values, and you may be neither loved nor popular. However, it is likely that you will be effective and respected. The world will be different in a better way because you have made the difficult choice to be something that is uncommon but desperately needed.

If you choose to be a superintendent, may your journey be one in which you rise to meet the challenges. Along the way, it may become difficult to sustain feelings of purpose and passion. People will reject your aspirations as too unrealistic, challenging, or disruptive. Results may arrive slowly. You may become frustrated by a discouraging reality. However, don't let your heart close up. When your career is finished, you will know that, by doing this difficult job in an ethical and professional way, your actions will ripple through time, leaving a better world behind you.

KEY POINTS OF THIS CHAPTER

- Great managers are not always great leaders. However, you have to do the management portion well to have the capacity to lead.
- True leaders adhere to a set of core values. Some of these values include:

  - Treat everyone with respect.
  - Do what you said you were going to do.
  - Be honest, yet tactful.
  - Follow your moral compass.
  - Take strategic risks.
  - Persevere.

- You may not always live up to the core values you believe in, but you owe it to yourself and others to strive to do so.
- You can make a difference in the world.

QUESTIONS FOR DISCUSSION OR REFLECTION

1. Why do you want to become or why are you currently serving as superintendent of schools? What is the reason you have that makes you want to do or continue doing this job?
2. Which of the core leadership values presented rings true for you? What others would you substitute? Are there any you would eliminate?

Bonus Truths

In this section, I share with you some additional truths that were not worth an entire chapter, but nonetheless are still valuable tips.

- You will never be right on decisions you make due to inclement weather. Some people will think you should close school, whereas others will think you should have remained open. When making decisions such as these, always do what is best for student safety, and err on the side of caution. Regardless of public sentiment or the outcomes, it is the right thing to do, and you will always be in the most legally defensible position.
- Because you don't teach or have direct contact with students, people assume that you don't do anything but collect a big paycheck. Until our professional associations make the importance of our roles and responsibilities clear to the public, avoid reading comments in print and on social media about our profession. The comments will depress you or make you angry.
- Special education costs can make or break the finances of a school district. It is a high priority to have an excellent director of special education and a high-quality special education attorney on retainer. In addition, learn as much as you can about special education law. You literally cannot afford to be clueless about this aspect of school district operations.
- Unless it is an emergency, try to avoid having staff and board members contact you at home after work hours. You need time to recharge and rejuvenate with loved ones. Do your best to leave your work at work. In addition, don't constantly check your work email from home. It may ruin your night, and most likely whatever it is can wait until morning.
- Regular physical exercise and a sense of humor are great antidotes to job stress. Work out regularly and laugh a lot. In addition, plan for and take

- your vacations. Sometimes, the greatest insights you will have will come when you take time to get away from the school district.
- While the actual phrasing may differ, the two words that characterize every appointment someone makes to see you are I want . . . Often, what they want is to take the monkey off their back and put it on yours. Don't let this happen, or you will always be responsible for solving everyone's problems.
- If at all possible, do not actively participate in collective bargaining sessions. Once the agreement is reached, you still have to work with those who were on the opposite side of the table.
- We never wish for a crisis, but, if you work in one place for a long enough period of time, they are inevitable. Importantly, moments of crises are often the defining moments for a leader. Within every crisis is the opportunity to demonstrate what makes you a leader. When a crisis occurs, you will be judged for what you do and how you handle yourself. In times of crisis, the role of the superintendent is heightened and moved to the forefront; be prepared and remember the importance of these moments.
- In general, there are two types of people who work in schools. First, there are those who are givers. These are the individuals who demonstrate the ability to genuinely express gratitude and personal concern. Second, there are takers. No matter how much you give them, takers never willingly give more of themselves than the minimum required. In addition, takers are either incapable of or unwilling to demonstrate appreciation. They take what they are given for granted. Do not give special privileges or extra attention to takers, thinking that they will appreciate it. There will be no payoff, only wasted energy. No matter how much you give to a taker, it will never be enough.
- Praise in public, criticize in private, and never gossip. You can never give too much authentic praise.

References

Ackerman, R. H., and P. Maslin-Ostrowski. 2002. *The Wounded Leader: How Real Leadership Emerges in a Time of Crisis*. San Francisco: Jossey Bass.
Bell, J. J. "Superintendent Job Satisfaction in an Era of Reduced Resources and Increased Accountability." *AASA Journal of Scholarship and Practice* 16, no. 3 (2019): 39–51.
Black, J. A., and F. W. English. 2001. *What They Don't Tell You in Schools of Education about School Administration*. Lanham, MD, and London: Scarecrow Press.
Coda, R., and R. Jetter. 2016. *Escaping the School Leader's Dunk Tank: How to Prevail When Others Want to See You Drown*. San Diego: Dave Burgess Consulting.
Dotlich, D. L., J. L. Noel, and N. Walker. 2004. *Leadership Passages: The Personal and Professional Transitions That Make or Break a Leader*. San Francisco: Jossey Bass.
Evert, T. F., and A. E. Van Deuren. 2013. *Thriving as a Superintendent: How to Recognize and Survive an Unanticipated Departure*. Lanham, MD, New York, Toronto, Plymouth, UK: Rowman & Littlefield.
Heifetz, R. A. 1994. *Leadership without Easy Answers*. Boston: Belknap Press.
Heifetz, R. A., and M. Linsky. 2002. *Leadership on the Line: Staying Alive through the Dangers of Leading*. Boston: Harvard Business School Press.
Hoyle, J. R., and L. Skrla. "The Politics of Superintendent Evaluation." *Journal of Personnel Evaluation in Education* 13, no. 4 (2019): 405–19.
Kowalski, T. J., and C. C. Brunner. "The School Superintendent: Roles, Challenges and Issues." *Educational Leadership Faculty Publications* 43 (2011).
Marzano, R. 2003. *What Works in Schools: Translating Research into Action*. Alexandria, VA: Association for Supervision and Curriculum Development.
Melton, T. D., L. T. Reeves, J. S. McBrayer, and A. Q. Smith. 2019. "Navigating the Politics of the Superintendency." *AASA Journal of Scholarship and Practice* 16, no. 3: 23–34.
Moffett, J. "Perceptions of School Superintendents and Board Presidents on Improved Pupil Performance and Superintendent Evaluation." *International Journal of Educational Leadership Preparation*, 2011 6(1), 1–7.
Polka, W. S., and P. R. Litchka. 2008. *The Dark Side of Educational Leadership: Superintendents and the Professional Victim Syndrome*. Lanham, MD, New York, Toronto, and Plymouth, UK: Rowman & Littlefield.
Spencer, M. 2013. *Exploiting Children: School Board Members Who Cross the Line*. Lanham, MD, New York, Toronto, and Plymouth, UK: Rowman & Littlefield.

About the Author

Matthew J. Jennings is a twenty-seven-year veteran of education. He has served as a superintendent, assistant superintendent, director of student services, supervisor of curriculum and instruction, and a classroom teacher. He earned his master's degree and doctorate in educational administration from Rutgers University.

In addition to presenting at numerous state and national conferences, Dr. Jennings has served as a consultant to school districts throughout New Jersey. He has taught as an adjunct professor for Rutgers University and the College of New Jersey. In addition to publishing books with the Association for Supervision and Curriculum Development, Corwin Press, and Rowman & Littlefield, his work has been published in *Kappan*, *Preventing School Failure*, *The New Jersey English Journal*, *Channels*, *The Writing Teacher*, and the *American School Boards Journal*.

When he is not spending time with his wife, MaryAnn, and his children, Ryan and Tara, Dr. Jennings enjoys time at the beach, exercising, and travel. He is looking forward to hiking the Appalachian Trail upon his retirement from public education.

www.ingramcontent.com/pod-product-compliance
Lightning Source LLC
Chambersburg PA
CBHW021215240426
43672CB00026B/324